The Enneagram Spectrum of Personality Styles

An Introductory Guide

Jerome P. Wagner, Ph.D.

Metamorphous Press
Portland, OR

Published by

Metamorphous Press
P.O. Box 10616
Portland, OR 97210-0616

Copyright © 1996 by Jerome P. Wagner, Ph.D.
Editorial and Art Direction by Lori Stephens
Printed in the United States of America

Wagner, Jerome P., 1941-
    The enneagram spectrum of personality styles / Jerome P. Wagner.
        p.   cm.
    Includes bibliographical references.
    ISBN 1-55552-070-7
    1. Enneagram. 2. Typology (Psychology) I. Title.
BF698.3.E54W34   1996
155.2'6—dc20   96-13484

Table of Contents

THE ENNEAGRAM SPECTRUM OF PERSONALITY STYLES

Foreword

by Helen Palmer

I first met Dr. Wagner through a microfilm of his dissertation over twenty years ago—an academic treatment of the Enneagram material that has recently attracted a wide international audience. Since then, we've conferred, argued, agreed, and challenged each other's thinking, all of which has been immensely satisfying. Even when you don't see eye to eye with Jerry, his clarity always adds an interesting angle to the debate.

This workbook is his piece of the Enneagram magic that draws those who seek something more than Freud's agenda of good love and work as the apex of well-being. It's a really good guide and I'm delighted to recommend it to both new and longterm students who will benefit from his way of bringing the types to life.

Helen Palmer
Teacher and author of *The Enneagram,*
The Enneagram In Love And Work,
The Pocket Enneagram

Foreword

by Thomas Condon

Most introductions to the Enneagram reduce it to a collection of types, but this book takes just the right tone. It offers a dynamic version of the system that is rooted in common sense and personal experience.

The writing is distilled and precise, and Wagner's descriptions of personality styles reflect his own vocabulary and vision. Deep mastery of the Enneagram is hard-won and evident in the quality of insight presented here; the author has decades of experience and it shows.

I especially like the book's exercises. Simple yet profound, they point directly to the Enneagram's best purpose—unveiling our inner map of reality. Readers will find surprising new ways to apply the Enneagram both personally and professionally as well as a direct path to their personal depths. For these and many other reasons, this book is a pleasure to recommend.

Thomas Condon
Author of *The Everyday Enneagram,*
The Enneagram Movie & Video Guide

Introduction

It is always fascinating and mutually confirming when theories and descriptions of personality from various sources of perennial wisdom resonate with contemporary psychological systems of personality. Such is the case with the Enneagram theory of the human person with its manifestations in nine personality styles.

The Enneagram is a nine-pointed figure in a circular setting that is used to display nine personality styles. (In Greek, *Ennea* means nine and *gramma* means point.)

This array has been compared to a wheel of colors. As you shine white light into a prism, it fans out into a spectrum of the basic colors. According to this metaphor, every person contains all the hues of the spectrum although one color particularly stands out or characterizes each individual. From a spiritual point of view, this metaphor says that Divinity descends and shows itself through nine earthly manifestations; from a philosophical point of view, it says that Being is disclosed through nine essential characteristics; from a psychological viewpoint, it states that human nature is expressed in nine natural fundamental ways.

The personality paradigms or patterns that are arranged in this circumplex model represent, depending on which metaphor you select, either nine manifestations of the Divine, or nine qualities of Being, or nine phenomenological world views and perspectives. From this latter point of view, these underlying fundamental schemas or maps are root organizing assumptions or core beliefs which influence and even determine our perceptions, thoughts, values, feelings, and behaviors. These paradigms are at the heart of how we think and feel about ourselves and other people and they govern the kinds of interactions with others we allow ourselves to think about and to have. These styles, then, are different ways of being in the world; different ways of experiencing, perceiving, understanding, evaluating, and responding to ourselves, others, and reality.

Traditional schools of wisdom often use a circle as a symbol of unity, completeness and fullness. So it is not surprising that a circular figure is used to describe the full range of human expression. Interestingly, modern psychology through complex statistical factor analysis has found that circumplex models are the most apt means for graphically plotting personality characteristics.

Although the origins of the Enneagram are disputed (some speculate its roots lie in antiquity; some trace its lineage to the middle ages; still others allege it is a modern discovery) and the exact transmission of the Enneagram symbol remains murky, what is clear is that the laws and descriptions of the human essence and personality as seen through the lens of the Enneagram have been recognized in some fashion across centuries as well as across races, cultures, age spans, and genders. There does appear to be something universal in the nature and functioning of the human person that is being expressed through this system.

Since it has become better known in the last twenty years, the Enneagram has become popular and is being validated in such varying cultures as Japan, India, Africa, Europe, North and South America. Today it is being used in a variety of settings from growth centers and therapy rooms to classrooms and business boardrooms with a variety of purposes from personal, psychological, and spiritual growth to couple interactions, team-building, and management effectiveness.

The Enneagram was originally transmitted through oral tradition and is probably best learned through hearing about it and interacting with others. Only in the last few years has the Enneagram been transcribed into written form for wider publication. This Introduction with its workbook and exercises is intended to be a bridge between the oral and written traditions. It can be used by workshop presenters, therapists, and consultants as a teaching aid for introducing the Enneagram to their clients. It can also stand on its own as a brief written primer for the Enneagram.

The exercises and descriptions that follow are designed to introduce you to the general personality theory that grounds the Enneagram and to familiarize you with the nine hues that make up its spectrum of personality styles. Hopefully this combination of experiential reflection and presentation of theory will help you locate, understand, and appreciate your own particular style.

This primer presumes no prior knowledge of the Enneagram. Complete the exercises in the Introduction, compare with your own style the word and phrase descriptors before each chapter, then consider the descriptions of the nine Enneagram styles.

The word/phrase descriptors are meant to be a *precis* or partial cataloging of the positive and negative features of the nine styles. For a formally researched, statistically reliable and validated inventory, with a standardized sample and normative scores, you might want to take the *Wagner Enneagram Personality Style Scales (WEPSS)* to help you to differentiate your type (now in the research and development phase).

Like the *WEPSS,* the exercises have been developed over many years, through many workshops and courses. They are designed to help you reflect on your own experience. As you till the data of your experience, the Enneagram descriptions may expose a pattern that has been present in your life without your recognizing it.

The exercises begin with very general reflection questions and then become more specific, something like a funnel which is wide at the top and narrow at the bottom. There are exercises for each dimension of the Enneagram personality mosaic. So this manual follows the process of knowing. Begin with your *experience* to provide the data; then let *understanding* arise from your experience to produce a template for organizing the data; then come to some *judgment* about your experience and understanding.

CORE SELF OR ESSENCE OR OBJECTIVE PARADIGM

Some schools of perennial wisdom (including the Enneagram) and some contemporary psychological theories of development and personality make a basic distinction between our *essence* or real self and our *personality* or public or false self. First we'll consider our natural, genuine core self—the self we were born with. Then we'll look at our public self—the protective covering around our true self that we donned and/or were conditioned into whose function is to protect our vulnerable self, keep it secure, and facilitate our commerce with our environment.

In our essence, at the heart of each style, lie certain strengths and capabilities that enable us to survive and thrive. We experience these abilities and qualities as values or ideals that we prize and are spontaneously drawn to. All of these values are virtually or potentially present in our core self, and we are capable of appreciating and actualizing all of them. Temperamentally, though, we tend to favor and are motivated by a hierarchy of these values, with one or a few being more potent and central than others. These values are the motivating and organizing tendencies that become central for each personality style. These *core value tendencies* organize and guide our energies, perceptions, emotional reactions, and behaviors. They are at the root of who we are and who we want to become.

The following exercises are designed to help you get in touch with your own core values. They are general inquiries into your fundamental attractions, orientations, meanings, and motivations. They are meant to reveal what is important to you, what really matters. Record your answers on a separate piece of paper or in a journal.*

Exercise 1—What is the purpose of life?

If a young child asked you what the purpose of life is—what are we here for—how would you respond to him or her? Re-

---

* A handy workbook is available for you to record your responses to these exercises—see pg. 136.

member, this is a young child (let's say around age six), so your response has to be simple and brief.

A variation of this theme would be to substitute a Martian for a child. The Martian asks you, as an Earthling, why you are on this planet. What is the purpose of Earthlings? What would you say to the Martian?

Take some time to reflect on this and record your answer.

Exercise 2—If you only had one year to live, what would you do?

If you were told you only had one year to live, what would you do in that year? Your health will be fine all the way up to the end. Then in the last few weeks you will deteriorate rapidly and die. How would you spend the year?

An additional consideration you might ask yourself is why aren't you doing this now? Why not now?

Exercise 3—Write your own personal mission statement.

What would you like or what do you understand your mission in life to be? This statement is meant to be the embodiment of your vision and values. This declaration will express what you believe the meaning of your life is all about.

Put another way: what is your vocation? What do you feel called *to be* and *to do*? What do you believe is the purpose of your life?

Write down your personal mission statement. Within it you will find expressed your innermost values and ideals (i.e., The kind of person I would like to be is____; The kinds of activities I would like to engage in are____; My personal mission is to____).

Exercise 4—What do you really want?

What do you *really* want in your truest self? Write down what comes to you.

With this material from your own experience and understanding, look now at Figure 1 (page 7).

Figure 1 summarizes much of the material that will be treated in discussing the nine Enneagram styles. Nine positive core characteristics or values are represented by the *innermost* circle (I) of Figure 1. These values are part of our essence. The healthy self has the potential for valuing, developing, and utilizing each of these characteristics. When one of these qualities is present, all are virtually present, for each contains the others. For example, if you cultivate the valued characteristic of goodness, you will also be loving, wise, loyal, and the rest. Pictorially, this is indicated by the dotted lines showing these core values as permeable and intermingling.

You will find these values described in more detail under the heading *Positive Core Value Tendencies* in the left hand column of each of the nine styles. If you compare your responses to Exercises 1, 2, 3, and 4 to the descriptions in this column, you may find some resonances to your own value preferences. The adjectives and phrases in the top section of each checklist titled *Positive Descriptions of Your Style* also point to the healthy characteristics found in the authentic self.

To operate effectively in the world, we need, and have available to us, all of these qualities. So in a situation when we need to be assertive, we can call on our power; when we need to be nurturing, we can call on our love; when we need to have fun, we can call on our joy, etc. The flexible person has this whole spectrum of adaptive attitudes and behaviors available. Even so, we naturally tend to rely on and use one or a few favorite ways of operating. By temperament or destiny we are particularly attracted to, are guided by, and cultivate one of these value vectors which becomes an organizer and expresser of the self. The other vectors are used as auxiliaries to complement our central preference.

We need all nine paradigm perspectives to see reality objectively. The healthy person has access to these reality based and reality informed paradigms which provide pliancy and flexibility to our style. To be effective, we need to take multiple perspectives on a problem or situation. Even so, we tend to see the world from one favored and developed perspective or another. This is the particular viewpoint, acumen and problem-solving

Enneagram Personality Style Profile

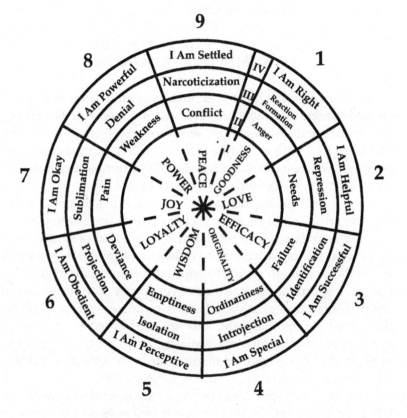

Figure 1

I Genuine Ideal or Authentic Values
II Area of Avoidance
III Defense Mechanism
IV Idealized Self-Image or Compensating Values

approach we have to offer any group. Due to our expertise in our paradigm, we can often perceive and understand some things more clearly than others; we are more competent in some areas than others; and we can resolve certain issues more easily than others. When we are acting from our healthy self, we contribute our strengths, gifts, and points of view to society.

PERSONALITY OR PUBLIC SELF
OR SUBJECTIVE PARADIGM

Under favorable inner and outer conditions and with good enough parenting, our core real self emerges and flourishes. When our spontaneous urges, sensations, feelings, images, and ideas are met with empathic interest, acceptance, and encouragement, we then develop according to the enfolding of our essential nature. We become who we really are.

However if the appearance of our core self is met with indifference, criticism, or misinterpretation, then we develop a personality or public self to cover our real self and protect it. This peripheral self is an attempt to defend and maintain our inner self in the face of our critics, to appease them, to gain their attention and approval, to win them over to our side, or to defeat them. These strategies are attempts to make ourselves attractive, good, acceptable, safe, and secure. Instead of *express*ing our real values, preferences, feelings, and thoughts, we try to *impress* others. We begin to manipulate both ourselves and others. We become what we believe we *have* to be.

Our core gifts get distorted and caricatured into ways we think we *should* be. To be acceptable or somebody, we *have* to be good, giving, efficient, special, etc. Our core ideals or values become crystallized into *idealized self-images,* partial expressions of our full self that we overidentify with and believe represent our whole self. We mistakenly believe that if we attain and manifest these idealizations, they will gain for us positive reinforcement or at least help us avoid negative reinforcement. Now we use our gifts and strengths to protect ourselves from others rather than to build up our community.

Our paradigms or perspectives on the world tend to become static, rigid, and inflexible. Our perspective becomes more limited and narrow and we develop tunnel vision. Our paradigms become distorted and subjective instead of reality-determined. We try to solve problems in the same stereotyped manner with the same automatic interpretations and reactions.

In sum, when we lose touch with our core self, we need to substitute something in its place. So we assume a personality and pursue substitute or compensating values in an attempt to fill in what feels missing.

Exercises 5 through 15 may help you discover your personality or subjective paradigm. These exercises explore the remaining three rings in Figure 1: your idealized self-image, an area you tend to avoid, and the defensive techniques you employ to help you avoid whatever doesn't fit your image of yourself.

Exercise 5—How have you survived?

In this "dog-eat-dog world," what advice would you give to a young child about how to survive? How do you make it in this cruel world? What kind of survival tactics and strategies have you discovered and devised that have kept you safe. For example, some people might suggest: "Get them before they get you." Others might say: "Be nice to people." While others might advise: "Get out of town or hide out."

Again, you may substitute a Venusian for a young child. Here the Venusian is asking how do Earthlings survive on this inhospitable planet? How have you managed to live this long?

Make a list of your techniques.

Exercise 6—Where have you been looking for what you want in the wrong places?

What have you substituted for what you really want that you wrote down in Exercise 4? As the song says, are you looking for love in all the wrong places (like in food, drink, or sex)? Or are you looking for truth through status? Etc.

Write down what you have settled for or have mistakenly been seeking.

Our idealized self-image or compensating values are represented by the *outermost* circle (IV) in Figure 1. These idealizations tend to be caricatures or exaggerations of the essential values and characteristics found in our real self. These personality styles lie around the periphery of our self where they act as a covering to protect the self and act as mediators or translators between the self and the world. These styles can vary in how flexible or stifling they are—and they vary in how well they translate or convey to the world who we really are and in how distorted or undistorted they bring in to us what is in the world. These strategies are demarcated by solid lines, indicating the rigidity and impermeability of the characteristics of our personality. The farther removed we get from our core self, the more stereotyped and automatic our thoughts, feelings, and behaviors become. The more set we are in our ways, the less the perspectives, approaches, and strengths of the other styles are available to us.

You will find these defensive or survival strategies for each of the nine styles spelled out more fully in the column entitled *Distorted Core Characteristics*. There you will see how our healthy strivings can become distorted when we overidentify with and overuse our basic gifts. Compare the survival techniques you cataloged in Exercises 5 and 6 with the ones listed here and see where you might recognize yourself.

AREA OF AVOIDANCE

Parts of ourselves we consider unacceptable, embarrassing, or intolerable because they don't fit our idealized self-image are disowned and relegated to our unconscious or are projected onto others. The result is that we lose touch with even more aspects of ourselves. Our response repertoire becomes more limited and, ultimately, we are less effective. The opposing attributes, polarities, or antitheses of our self-image, then, are found in our area of avoidance.

Each personality paradigm is like a lens or a searchlight with a particular focus and clarity. Those aspects of reality that lie outside the territory scanned by our paradigm are often vague, obscurely recognized, or not seen at all. Just as our paradigm enables us to see some things more clearly than others might, so we can miss or pass over realities and possibilities because we're not looking for them, are looking the other way, or don't want to see them.

Exercise 7—Me and Not-Me

Make two columnar lists. In the first column, write down all the characteristics you associate with yourself. These are qualities that you identify with, find acceptable, and place inside your self boundary.

In the next column, write down the opposite characteristics of the qualities you listed in the first column. These are the polarities you find unacceptable and don't want to identify with and so place outside your self boundary. You may repress these characteristics so they appear in your dreams as shadow figures. Or you may project them onto other people so they appear as traits you don't like in others or as traits you admire in others. You can project out or throw away your strengths as well as your weaknesses.

For example, in Column 1 (Me) you may have written: "I am nice." In Column 2 (Not-Me) you might write: "I am cruel," or whatever the opposite of nice might be for you.

In the first column (Me) you may have said: "I am fearful," or "I seek security." While in the second column (Not-Me) you may have said: "I am brave," or "I am adventuresome," or whatever the polarity of fearful and security-seeking is for you.

Exercise 8—Reowning the Not-Me

Go back to your list of characteristics in Column 2 and identify with them or reown them. For example, how are you cruel? Or brave? Resist your initial reaction of saying "I'm not," and search out areas of your life where you have or do now manifest these qualities. They represent untapped energy and strength. If you can access them, they will broaden your paradigm considerably and give you more resources for handling situations that arise.

Exercise 9—Reframing the Not-Me

If you're still having trouble identifying with some characteristics in your Not-Me column, take each quality and think about what good is in that characteristic. For example, what's good about being cruel? Or what good qualities are contained in being cruel? Perhaps these good qualities are being distorted. For example, there might be considerable strength contained in the anger and aggression found in being cruel. If this strength and energy can be tapped cleanly, you can use it productively.

Exercise 10—What are you afraid of?

What fears stand between you and your real self? What are your fears that are keeping you from doing what you really want to do?

What is the demon or dragon that guards the path to your inner self? When you quiet yourself and attempt to get in touch with yourself, what arises to distract you or block your view?

Make a list of all the things you are afraid of.

Exercise 11—How do your fears keep you trapped in your false personality or ego?

Often we become stuck in our habitual patterns of thinking, feeling, and behaving because our irrational and no longer helpful fears get in the way of trying something new and different.

For example, do you always have to be nice and accommodating because you are afraid of expressing your anger or your opinion for fear that people will not like you?

Or do you always have to be working on some project for fear that if you slow down or have nothing to do, some uncomfortable feelings or wishes may arise in you? Or are you afraid there will be no one there when you finally come home to yourself?

Consider the fears you catalogued in Exercise 10. Notice how they keep you imprisoned in your recurring reaction loops, and determine whether these fears are still realistic or mostly mythical by now.

Exercise 12—Where are the edges of your paradigm?

Does your own paradigm create certain perceptions, inter-pretations, rules, limits, boundaries, or taboos that keep you fear-ful?

For example, if your paradigm involves perfectionism, then your rules say you have to be right all the time and you fear being wrong or not doing something perfect enough. Someone with a different paradigm won't be bothered nearly as much about being right or exact. Or if your paradigm says you have to look calm, cool, and collected in order to survive, then you "can't" express your feelings and you are afraid of them and stay away from them. On the other hand, someone else can express their feelings freely, but they're not allowed to think straight.

Paradigms involve strong beliefs, and when you come up to the edge of your belief, it can be very frightening to go any far-ther. For example, if you believe the world is flat, when you come up to your horizon you won't want to go any further.

So, if you believe you have to be strong, then you might be afraid of and avoid being weak.

Write out how your paradigm creates your fears and avoid-ances and how the rules of your paradigm prohibit you from doing what you legitimately might want to do.

Exercise 13—If you break this rule or taboo or cross this bound-ary, what are you afraid will happen?

Taboos or idols have power because you make yourself afraid of them.

What are you telling yourself or what have you been told happens to people who possess this dreaded quality or who manifest these terrible characteristics? What will happen to you if you go too far?

What happens to people who get angry? Are they shunned, abandoned, locked up?

What happens to people who are lazy? Do they turn out to be bums? Or do they end up like your Uncle Harry or your older sister?

Are the consequences specific ("You'll be sent to the insane asylum") or vague? ("You'd better not do that, or else!")

Write down what you are afraid will happen if you enter your area of avoidance.

Exercise 14—What do you need to do to stop worshipping this idol? What do you need to cast out this fear? What resources do you need to marshal to confront your fears?

Perhaps you need to turn around and confront your fear. Maybe all dogs (or men or women) don't bite. Expose yourself to the very thing you are afraid of. You may be surprised to discover that you survive.

Perhaps you need to upgrade your information or get information you lack. Sex may not make your hair fall out or permanently stain your soul. The information you initially received which made you fearful may have been faulty.

Perhaps before you say goodbye, you may first need to reassure yourself that you will have connections in the future. Or before you make contact, you may need to feel the inner strength to be able to break that contact and withdraw when you need to.

You may need to rally some inner allies before you face your fears and/or you might want some outer friends and guides around when you push through your fear barrier. You don't necessarily have to do all it by yourself.

Write down the strategies and resources you already have and those you may need to acquire.

This land of shadows or area of avoidance is represented by circle II of Figure 1. Notice that it lies between the core self and the personality. The most direct route to the self is through this avoided territory. To find ourselves we need to look at, identify with, reclaim, and repatriate these banished features of our self. The way to wholeness is through honoring and integrating all of our polarities, not through cutting off half of them. Holding onto both ends of our polarities creates energy; letting go of one end depletes energy.

You will also find a section describing the *Area of Avoidance* under each of the nine Enneagram styles. Compare these with your own avoidances you discovered in Exercises 7-14 and see where you recognize yourself.

DEFENSE MECHANISMS

As we approach our area of avoidance, we become anxious. So we devise ways to keep these unacceptable aspects of ourselves out of our awareness. The defense mechanisms act as buffers between our *persona* or idealized self and our shadow characteristics or avoided self. Whatever we consider to be *I* is allowed inside our paradigm or personality boundary and is granted access to our awareness. What we think of as *Not-I* is placed outside our paradigm boundary and is banished from consciousness. Our defenses prevent these rejected aspects of ourselves from entering the province of the personality. Unfortunately, they also keep us from contacting and reowning these parts of our core self.

Exercise 15—What are your defense mechanisms?

This is a difficult question, because if your defense mechanisms are working properly, you won't be aware of them—so you need to be patient and observe yourself carefully.

When you start to feel anxious, what happens next? What do you do?

When you vaguely become aware of something in yourself you are uncomfortable with (like feeling angry, afraid, sexy, etc.) or if someone else brings up something you are uncomfortable with, what do you do to avoid it? For example, do you distract yourself or change the subject? Do you go blank and lose your train of thought, stop feeling, numb out, tighten your muscles, or hold your breath?

Do you go into your head and get too heady? Or do you lose your mind and get too feeling? Or do you just act impulsively without much thought or feeling?

Do you blame others and start finding fault with them?

Do you do the opposite of what you really want to do? If you want to do something for yourself, do you do what you *should* do instead? Or if you want to slug someone, are you nice to them instead?

Do you repress or deny what seems to be quite obvious to others?

You probably have many defense mechanisms at your disposal. We need them to survive psychologically. Write down the ones you rely on the most.

The defense mechanisms are found in circle III of Figure 1, between the idealized self-image (circle IV) and the area of avoidance (circle II). Graphically, the defense mechanisms separate what we identify with as ourself from what we avoid as antithetical to our self. Psychically, they serve the same buffering function.

You will also find a characteristic *Defense Mechanism* described under each of the nine Enneagram styles. Notice whether any of the defenses you discovered in Exercise 15 match any of these.

OBJECTIVE PRINCIPLES AND
PARADIGMS / ADAPTIVE COGNITIVE SCHEMAS

Just as our physical body has certain laws and principles by which it operates, so does the psyche have certain laws within which it functions optimally. As the body has certain tolerances or limits within which we must stay or we damage the body (i.e., our body temperature can only go so high or so low or we might die), so does the psyche have certain boundaries that need to be respected or we injure the psyche (i.e., we can only tolerate so much injustice, unloving, ugliness, etc. before we become sick in our spirit or demoralized.)

When we are living in accordance with our core authentic self, we have an intuitive, though perhaps unconscious, understanding of these objective principles or natural laws. Our paradigms or inner maps are accurate reflections of reality and are reliable guides for our choices and behaviors because they are aligned with the laws of the universe and with the laws of our own human nature. We function most effectively when we live in harmony with these universal principles. They are built-in to lead us to self-realization, to self-transcendence, and to communion with others and the world.

These objective principles and paradigms are found in the *inner* circle of Figure 2 where they reside in our essence or real self. These attitudes are delineated by dotted lines, indicating their mutual co-presence and influence. That is, each of these principles implies and virtually contains all the others. For example, when freedom is present, there is also hope, justice, love, etc.

Schemas represent patterned ways of thinking, feeling, and behaving. Adaptive cognitive schemas faithfully record, code, and organize external and internal data, so our cognitive maps are accurate reflections of the territory. They are formulated on repetitions occurring in the real world. They are adaptive because they enable us to realistically negotiate our way around in the world.

You will find these objective paradigms or adaptive schemas described under the heading *Adaptive Cognitive Schemas* for each of the nine Enneagram styles. Each style has a particular principle that is especially useful to remember and operate out of so the person remains aligned with reality and her or his own true nature.

Exercise 16—When you are in a resourceful state, what beliefs are in place that align you with reality?

When you hold and express certain beliefs, attitudes, and assumptions, you will find your body feeling physically relaxed, supple, strong, and energetic. You will experience genuine emotions such as joy, sadness, anger, fear, etc. Your mind will be clear, open, and expansive.

Since it might be difficult to uncover these underlying objective paradigms or principles, work backwards. Recall a moment when you felt at home and at ease in your body, when you spontaneously felt and expressed some feeling, when you were attentive, alert, clearheaded and singleminded, when you genuinely felt connected to yourself and others; in short, when you were fully present in the here and now.

In this resourceful state, what adaptive beliefs did you have about yourself, about others, about the world and your place in it?

Record your underlying perceptions, beliefs, and principles.

SUBJECTIVE OR DISTORTING PARADIGMS/ MALADAPTIVE COGNITIVE SCHEMAS

When we lose touch with our core self and lose faith in our inner and outer reality, we fashion our own vision and version of reality. Our narrowed and inflexible paradigms or faulty assumptions and belief systems are inaccurate maps which limit and distort our perception of reality. They are not trustworthy guides since they lead to the self-defeating strategies of the personality (though they were originally hoped to be self-protecting and enhancing). When we follow these disordered perceptions, feelings, and behaviors, we are on the path away from our core self and away from genuine contact with others.

Maladaptive schemas impose archaic patterns on reality. They recreate and then perceive old repetitions and recurrences where there may not be any. They are maladaptive because these maps don't fit the contemporary territory but rather distort incoming information to fit old patterns.

These illusory paradigms or perceptions and their ensuing limited strategies are found in the *outer* circle of Figure 2 where they reside in the periphery or *personality*. These stances are separated by solid lines, indicating their narrow focus and tunnel vision. These positions often exclude other points of view.

You will find these distorting paradigms spelled out under the heading *Maladaptive Cognitive Schemas* for each of the nine styles. Each style has a particular trap or maladaptive schema that keeps the individual stuck in a recurring reaction loop.

Exercise 17—When you are in a non-resourceful state, what are the distorted perceptions and inaccurate interpretations that are in place then?

When you hold beliefs and assumptions that are not aligned with your own true nature or with reality, you will experience

Adaptive and Maladaptive Cognitive Schema of Each Personality Style

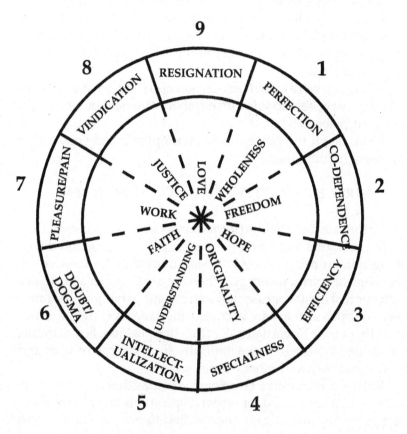

CORE (inner circle) =
Adaptive Schema/Objective Paradigm
PERIPHERY (outer circle) =
Maladaptive Schema/Distorting Paradigm

Figure 2

your body being tense, rigid, enervated or hyperactive; you will experience contaminated feelings such as guilt, depression, hostility, envy, greed; your mind will be distracted, closed, cluttered, confused.

Remember a time when you felt disconnected from yourself and from others, when your body felt anxious and tense, when your emotions felt crabbed or numbed or out of control, when your mind couldn't focus or when you couldn't get it off something; in short, when you were in the "there and then" instead of in the present.

When you were in that non-resourceful state, what were your maladaptive beliefs about yourself, about others, about the world and your place in it?

Write down the perceptions, assumptions and convictions you were holding then.

VIRTUES/ADAPTIVE EMOTIONAL SCHEMAS

Virtues are good habits (*virtus* means strength in Latin). They are the strengths that accompany a fully functioning and developing human being. They are clear, undistorted, objective expressions of spiritual energy. When we are living in accordance with our real nature or essential self and our paradigms, assumptions and perceptions are accurate and objective, then a corresponding virtue flows naturally from this position. For example, the virtue of courage flows naturally from a sense of faith and trust in our own and others' inner nature.

Virtues are adaptive emotional schemas that emanate from our essential nature and represent dispositions that manifest our best self. They are attitudes best suited to help us connect and harmonize with reality and to energize, fulfill, and transcend our real self.

The *inner* circle of Figure 3 displays the virtues of each type. They are the endowments of our essence. They are separated by a dotted line, indicating that when one of the virtues is present, all the others are in effect contained within it.

You will also find a characteristic *Virtue* or *Adaptive Emotional Schema* detailed in the left hand column for each of the nine Enneagram styles. Just as each style has a particular objective principle or adaptive cognitive schema to align you with and remind you of your true nature, each style also has a distinctive virtue or guiding force and attitude to keep you on your true path.

Exercise 18—What are the virtues or strengths or good habits needed for living a balanced adult life?

In your opinion, what skills and dispositions does a person need to live in an adult manner?

For example, what interpersonal or social skills should a person cultivate and possess? What intellectual, emotional, physical, moral, spiritual competencies does a person need for a sense of adult efficacy and mastery? Write out your list.

Look at the nine virtues presented for the Enneagram styles. Did any of them surprise you? Did you leave any of them out of your list? You might want to add them.

Considering all the virtues and skills mentioned, which ones do you already possess and are adept at?

Which habits and skills are you missing or deficient in?

What is interfering with your possessing and developing these virtues? For example, do you have some prohibition or inhibition about being strong? or loving? or feeling? or humorous? or intelligent?

You might also want to look ahead to the next section. Perhaps there is some bad habit or passion in place and operating that prevents the virtue from appearing and functioning.

PASSIONS/MALADAPTIVE EMOTIONAL SCHEMAS

Passions are bad habits. They are distorted expressions of spiritual energy which try to substitute for the virtues. Passions fuel and inflate the personality but do not nourish our core self, so we never feel really satisfied after exercising or giving into them. A self-defeating cycle gets established between our distorting paradigm and idealized self-image and the ruling passion. The idealized self-image inevitably gives rise to the passion which in turn urges us to pursue the automatic thoughts and behaviors of the personality. So each of the nine subjective paradigms produces its characteristic passion. For example, the pursuit of perfection, wherein we compare everything to unattainable ideals and then attempt to reach those ideals, leads to resentment because nothing appears as right or as fair as it should be. This anger and resentment then drive us to try harder to be perfect. Just as we tend to have only one idealized self-image, so each of us tends to have a basic ruling passion or vice.

Passions are maladaptive emotional schemas since they arise from the false self or personality, represent our non-resourceful self, and don't lead to satisfying contact between our real self and the world.

The passions and virtues are mutually opposing. If, in the presence of your passion, you simply observe it and don't act on it, then you experience your virtue. For example, if you feel greedy, but don't grab, then you are practicing the virtue of detachment.

Because the passions are associated with the peripheral self or personality, they are found in the *outer* circle of Figure 3. They are represented by solid lines since the passions tend to operate in a blind and inflexible manner with a tunnel-vision urgency.

The *Passions* or *Maladaptive Emotional Schemas* are also delineated in the right hand column (across from and opposed to the Virtues) for each of the nine Enneagram styles.

Exercise 19—What passions are in possession of you?

The passions are experienced as an addictive energy. They feel like alien forces that drive you and that seem out of your control.

What are the addictions and urges of your personality? What are you driven to thinking and feeling and doing that you know really isn't good for you? For example, do you compulsively compare yourself to others? Do you feel possessed by resentment or vengeance that you can't (or won't) let go of? Do you *have* to have something and feel desperately bad if you missed it?

Write down your addictions, compulsions, obsessions, blind

Adaptive and Maladaptive Emotional Schema of Each Personality Style

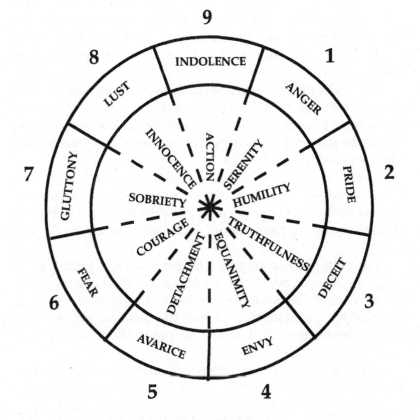

CORE (inner circle) = Adaptive Schema/Virtue
PERIPHERY (outer circle) = Maladaptive Schema/Passion

Figure 3

urges, desires, thoughts, judgments, etc. Then compare these with the passions described for the Enneagram styles and note any similarities.

Exercise 20—What is your predominant fault?

According to perennial wisdom and many religious traditions, the passion was referred to as your predominant fault or cardinal sin since it was from this source or "hinge" that all your other misdirected attitudes and behavior flowed or were connected.

Do any of the passions or addictions you noted seem central to your personality style? Do any of these mal-energized attitudes seem to cause most of your problems? Do you recognize any of the passions as being pervasive throughout your personality or paradigm distortions?

Consider how this passion influences your perceptions, choices, and behaviors. Trace the tendrils of this passion throughout the fabric of your personality. Like the roots of a weed, you need to see how it stretches out and touches much of what you do.

For example, if your predominant passion is gluttony, you might note how your desire for new and varied experiences to spice up your life, your need to have your options open and commitments contained, your fear and avoidance of pain, etc. are all manifestations of your basic predominant fault or passion.

Write down your reflections and observations about your predominant fault.

PARADIGM SHIFTS

The following exercises are designed to help you reflect on changes in your perceptions, feelings, and behaviors. You may experience these shifts either as voluntary choices or involuntary movements. Hopefully you will gain some insights into how to vary your customary manner of interacting. The next exercise proposes the fundamental paradigm shift query.

Exercise 21—What is impossible for you to do within your own style? What can't you imagine yourself doing (i.e., if you could or would do it, it would fundamentally change your style)?

A paradigm shift takes you outside of your own boundaries and into another paradigm or worldview with a new set of rules and boundaries.

What you find difficult to do might be relatively easy inside another paradigm. If your paradigm makes it difficult for you to express your feelings, another paradigm might make it natural and expected. If your paradigm makes expressing anger difficult for you, another's paradigm might make it facile. Or if your paradigm makes clear thinking difficult, another paradigm will find it the logical thing to do.

Some problems can't be easily solved by your paradigm but can be solved by someone else's paradigm. You can find the answers to some of your "unsolvable problems" by applying someone else's paradigm.

For example, do you find it hard to imagine yourself doing first what you want to do and then second what you *should* do? Or vice versa?

Do you find it almost inconceivable that you would express your feelings openly as you are feeling them?

Does it seem unimaginable to you to live without doubts?

Write down what you can't do (or, really, won't allow yourself to do)—something which, if you were doing it, would be a radical change in your style of living and interacting.

Exercise 22—What happens to you under stressful conditions?

Do you find yourself regressing to earlier patterns of behavior? Do you find yourself thinking, feeling, behaving the way you did when you were little?

Do you try other desperate measures to avoid dealing with your issues?

Or under stress do you sometimes rise to the occasion and surprise yourself by how well you cope under pressure or in an emergency? Do you rally resources in yourself you usually don't call up?

Paradigm Shifts

I am settled /
Conflict
9.

I am powerful / 8.
Weakness

I am good /
Anger

I am O.K. / 7.
Pain

2. I am helpful /
Needs

I am loyal / 6.
Deviancy

3. I am successful /
Failure

I am wise / 5.
Emptiness

4. I am special /
Ordinariness

Movements Toward Resourceful
and Non-Resourceful States

Figure 4

Write down what you're like when you fall apart under stress. What are you thinking, feeling, and doing when you start to disintegrate? When stress brings out the worst in you, just what is that worst?

Write down what you're like when you pull yourself together under stress. How do you respond gracefully under fire? What are your effective coping strategies when you're under pressure? What are you thinking, feeling, and doing when you rise to the occasion?

STRESSFUL CONDITIONS

Under stress, each style tends towards certain backup strategies of defense and coping. When our customary automatic paradigms and emotional and behavioral patterns fail to remedy the situation, we often compulsively use them more rather than try something different. When we finally give up on these patterns, or when they break down, we find ourselves by default using the compulsive maneuvers of another style.

Shifting to the Low Side of the Proceeding Style

This regressive backup strategy can be identified by following the direction of the arrow *forward* from our customary style to the *proceeding* style. We begin to take on and resemble the negative features or the *low side* of this type. Besides assuming the compulsive strategies of this style, we also start to shun the same aspects of reality this type avoids. Thus even more parts of ourselves become unavailable and our reactions become more narrow and rigid. For example, the sensitive person despairs of trying to be special, begins to avoid his or her own needs, and instead attempts to help others as a way to gain love and attention. S/he becomes a "suffering servant." This would be how Style 4 might move toward the low or compulsive side of Style 2 when experiencing inner and outer stress.

Shifting to the High Side of the Proceeding Style

Stress often brings out the worst in us. However, sometimes it brings out the best. Under these circumstances, we find ourselves deliberately choosing the alternate paradigm and effective methods of another style. We can shift to the *high side* of the proceeding style. For example, the sensitive person, realizing s/he is becoming overly self-absorbed or involved in her own process, elects to go out of herself and genuinely empathize and serve others. This would be how Style 4 under stress might move toward the high or healthy side of Style 2.

These paradigm shifts toward regression, fragmentation, and compulsion or toward growth, integration, and wholeness are diagrammed in Figure 4.

Look at the section *Paradigm Shifts You May Experience Under Stressful Conditions* for each of the nine Enneagram styles and see where you recognize some of your own pattern shifts under stress.

Exercise 23—What are you like in relaxed, nonthreatening situations?

When you are at your best, how do you *think* and *feel* about yourself, about other people, and about the way you can interact with others? How are you different here from when you feel anxious, threatened, or bad about yourself? What do you *do* when you are at your best that you can't or won't do at your worst?

When you feel safe (for example in your home environment or with your family) what do you allow yourself to think, feel, and do that you don't allow yourself to do in public? For example, are you more demanding or whining at home? Sometimes in familiar, comfortable settings, we allow our less sociably acceptable parts to come out.

Under relaxed conditions either some suppressed strengths or some covered up weaknesses may emerge.

Write down what you're like at your best when you feel safe, accepted, relaxed, integrated, free, and alive.

Now write down what you're like when you feel safe and

unthreatened and you let out the little gremlin or devil in you. What uncharacteristic or unsocial behaviors do you let yourself get away with?

HEALTHY CONDITIONS

Under relaxed, affirming conditions, each style tends toward more balanced, integrated, objective, proactive (vs. reactive) modes of perception and behavior. To remedy a situation, we *give in* to another approach instead of *giving up* on our customary approach. This represents a paradigm shift. We enlarge our perspective with another frame of reference and increase our behavioral repertoire with another set of skills.

Shifting to the High Side of the Preceding Style

This alternate paradigm and strategy is found in the healthy coping patterns of the style *preceding* our own, going *backward* against the direction of the arrow. We begin to assume and activate the positive features or *high side* of this type. To discover the underutilized resources in ourselves, we can look to the perspective, strengths, effective coping strategies, and attitudes of the preceding style to know what to draw upon in ourselves to get balanced or unstuck. It is generally healthy and motivating to be able to acknowledge and activate the idealized self statement of the preceding type. For example, it is beneficial for the perfectionist style to be able to say, "I'm okay even though I'm not perfect."

Shifting to the Down Side of the Preceding Style

Sometimes when we are in relaxed comfortable surroundings we can slip into the *down side* of the preceding style. We miss the mark and take on the compulsive features of the other paradigm. We do things in our family that we wouldn't dare do in public. For example, when feeling safe, the wise person might become bossy or cruel (the low side of Style 8) instead of acting out of their instincts and being assertive (the high side of Style 8).

These paradigm shifts toward growth, integration, and wholeness or towards stagnation, fragmentation, and compulsion are diagrammed in Figure 4.

Look at the descriptions of the *Paradigm Shifts You May Experience Under Relaxed Conditions* for each of the nine Enneagram styles and see where you recognize your perceptual, emotional, and behavioral shifts when you feel accepted and safe.

THREE CENTERS OR INSTINCTS

According to some schools of perennial wisdom, each person has three centers of intelligence or three loci of decision-making or three instincts that help us survive and thrive in the physical, interpersonal, and spiritual realms in which we live. Modern neuroanatomy has uncovered three layers in the evolution of the brain. There is the reptilian brain located atop the brain stem. Next developed the old mammalian brain consisting of the limbic system which encircles the reptilian brain. Finally, there evolved the neocortex which surrounds the mammalian brain.

The *instinct for self-preservation* is located in our gut center in the pelvic basin and provides us with a *physical sense* of how we are doing in relation to ourselves. It naturally informs us about what we need. When this instinct is ill-functioning or damaged, we experience a deep insecurity about ourselves. This is called the *Kath* center. In traditional wisdom, it is the place we go to get centered and still. It is also the center of movement as in Tai Chi and the martial arts. Various breathing, movement, and postural exercises are used to activate this center. In the reptilian brain are found those brain functions responsible for breathing, coordinating and smoothing movements, along with other autonomic nervous system activities. This section of the brain is said to contain the ancestral lore of the species.

The *instinct for interpersonal relations* is located in our heart center and provides us with an *emotional sense* of whom we are with and how we are doing in relationship to others. It tells us what the other person needs. When this instinct is not functioning, we experience a sense of loneliness. This is called the *Oth* center. In traditional wisdom, this is the center of devotion and love. The heart center is often activated by chanting or other auditory practices such as vocal prayer. The old mammalian brain contains those parts of the brain that regulate the emotions along with the pleasure/pain center.

The *instinct for connection and orientation* (syntony) is located in our head center and provides us with an *intellectual sense* of where we are, where we have come from, and where we are going. This instinct helps us find a sense of direction, purpose, and meaning. When it is damaged, we feel unconnected, useless, and inadequate. This is called the *Path* center. In perennial wisdom, the head center is activated through visualization techniques. This is the seat of enlightenment. The neocortex or gray matter is also called the associative cortex because it is able to make associations, plan ahead and consider consequences, delay and inhibit, make voluntary movements and carry on discourse with the external environment.

While each of us has and needs all three centers, we typically rely on and prefer one center over the others. Enneagram Types 8-9-1 prefer the *gut* center; Types 2-3-4 prefer the *heart* center; Types 5-6-7 prefer the *head* center. When one center tries to do the work of the other centers, we often become unbalanced and become too heady or too feeling dominated or too impulsive. When all three centers are allowed to function freely and work in harmony, we experience a sense of wholeness, integration, and balance.

Plato and later Gurdjieff spoke of three types of individuals in whom either the head, heart, or abdominal centers predominated. A fourth type of person was one who had integrated all three centers. Plato used the image of a winged chariot pulled by horses and driven by a charioteer to describe the interrelationships among the physical center (the chariot), the emotional center (the horses), and the intellectual center (the charioteer). Gurdjieff updated this image to his time and spoke of a carriage, horse, and driver to illustrate the three centers.

These three centers for gathering, evaluating, and acting on information are depicted in Figure 5.

The Three Instincts

Intellectual Center
Orienting instinct "Where am I?"
Purpose, direction
Dysfunction: Feels useless, inadequate

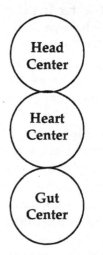

Emotional Center
Relating instinct "Who am I with?"
Social relationships
Dysfunction: Loneliness

Instinctual Center
Conserving instinct "How am I?"
Self preservation
Dysfunction: Insecurity about self

Figure 5

The remaining exercises ask you to reflect on your experience of your three centers.

Exercise 24—Which is your preferred center: head, heart, or gut (body)?

When you need to make an important decision, which center do you ultimately consult and trust?

Do you consult and trust logic and reason? Do you list the pros and cons of the various options available to you? Do you take a rational approach to decision-making? Do you use your head?

Do you consult and trust your emotions to discern how you feel about your various options? Do you imagine the possibilities available to you and let your feelings move you one way or the other? Do you use your heart?

Do you consult and trust your body to give you a felt sense for what you want? Do you make decisions rapidly and instinctively, sometimes before you think or feel anything about your options? With this judgment there seems no room for doubt. Do you use your gut?

Write out how you characteristically make important decisions in your life. You may find you use all three approaches. The more the better. But which center is your final "go ahead with it" arbiter?

Exercise 25—What is the condition of your carriage (physical center) at this time?

Have you taken care of your body or carriage? Is it polished and well-oiled and ready for the road of life? Or have you neglected it so it is rusty and can barely move?

Through exercise and movement, your muscles and joints naturally lubricate themselves. Do you regularly exercise to keep your body in tone?

Are you overweight so your horses can barely pull you? Or are you underweight to such an extent that you can't bear any burden placed on you?

Do you need to consider your diet? Are you providing your body the vitamins and minerals it needs? Or are you clogging up your arteries? If your body craves proteins, do you give it the nourishment it needs or do you feed it cotton candy?

Are addictions to food, drink, chemicals, smoking, etc. substituting for healthy bodily care?

Do you need to pursue any body therapies to get your carriage in shape (therapeutic massage, Rolfing, bioenergetics, Feldenkrais movement therapy, Reichian therapy, Reiki therapy, Tai Chi, Aikido or other martial arts, breathing therapies, Zen or other methods, to name just a few, for reaching your still point)?

Write down your reflections.

Exercise 26—What is the condition of your horses (emotional center) at this time?

What is the status of your emotional life? Have you developed your emotions to the extent you have developed your mind and body? Are you in touch with and comfortable expressing the full range of your feelings?

How are you with your *hard feelings* such as anger? Are you able to move against others with assertive and confrontational behavior?

How are you with your *soft feelings* such as love, affection and joy? Can you move towards others with warmth?

How are you with your *fragile feelings* such as sadness, embarrassment, and fear? Can you move away from others when appropriate? Or express your vulnerability?

Are your horses underfed and underexercised? Do you provide them with energy and oxygen? Or do you cut them off by holding your breath and tightening your muscles? Are your feelings overcontrolled, restricted, repressed, compulsive?

Or are your horses wild and undisciplined? Do your feelings run wild so they are in control of you instead of you providing a gently guiding rein? Are your feelings hysterical, labile, overwhelming, impulsive?

Again, are any addictions (food, alcohol, nicotine, chemical substances, people, work, etc.) substituting for, covering over, or distracting you from genuine emotional contact and expression?

Do you need to consider any emotional cathartic therapies to free your emotions? Examples include Gestalt therapy, group therapy, Primal Scream or other regressive therapies.

Write down how you are with your feelings.

Exercise 27—What is the condition of your driver (head center) at this time?

What is the status of your cognitive life? The fanciest carriage with the liveliest horses won't do you any good if your driver is drunk or doesn't know the way.

Are your cognitive maps, your belief systems, your assumptions, your ways of construing and interpreting reality accurate and up to date? or are you still working with the beliefs, attitudes, and maps you developed when you were a child? Do you need to update your maps?

Have you checked your assumptions out with other people lately? And have you checked your hypotheses and schemas against both external data and the data of your own experience? You may be changing the data to fit your schema or denying your own experience to fit some "should" or prejudice passed on to you when you were young.

Is your thinking clear or muddled? Are you engaging in "Stinkin' Thinkin'" as the Twelve-Step program calls it? Do you overgeneralize, absolutize, think in all-or-nothing, either-or, black-or-white categories? Do you minimize or ignore the data in front of you? Do you confuse your projections with reality?

Does your attention habitually go in a certain direction? or in a self-defeating cycle? Do you need some form of cognitive therapy to get your thinking up-to-date, accurate, and realistic? Rational-Emotive therapy, cognitive-behavioral or cognitive dynamic therapy, aspects of Neurolinguistic Programming, and Multi-Modal therapy are a few examples.

Write down your assessment of how your head center is functioning.

An earlier exercise (3) asked what you really wanted in your truest self. The remaining exercises ask you to be more specific and reflect on what each center of your self desires.

Exercise 28—What does your head need and want?

Exercise 29—What does your heart need and want?

Exercise 30—What does your gut (body) need and want?

The Nine Styles

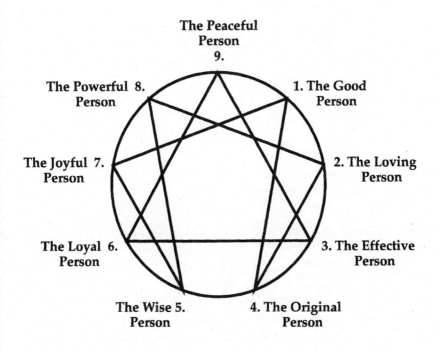

The Peaceful
Person
9.

The Powerful 8.
Person

1. The Good
Person

The Joyful 7.
Person

2. The Loving
Person

The Loyal 6.
Person

3. The Effective
Person

The Wise 5.
Person

4. The Original
Person

Style 1
The Good
Person

Positive Descriptors of Your Style

serious

responsible

dedicated

conscientious

high purpose

precise

punctual

honest

hardworking

moral

high standards

striving for excellence

idealistic

reliable

thorough

painstaking

fair

persevering

develop all potentials

ethical

clarity seeking

intense

Negative Descriptors of Your Style

overly critical

demanding

angry

uptight

sharp

driven

impatient

slave-driver

moralistic

trying too hard

perfectionistic

high expectations

unrealistic

overly-persistent

strict

interfering

puritanical

preachy

many "shoulds"

overly serious

Positive Core Value Tendencies	Distorted Core Characteristics
You value and are attracted to *goodness*. You want to make the world a better place to live in. You want to realize all of your potentials and help others actualize theirs.	You can overidentify with the *idealized self-image* of being *good, right, or perfect*. These become more important than anything else. If you are a good girl or good boy, then you are acceptable.
You have an appreciation for and a dedication to excellence and doing things well.	You are afraid to do anything unless you can do it perfectly.
You have an ability to see how people or situations could be and you are willing to work hard to bring about that reality.	You have difficulty accepting yourself, other people, and reality as it is.
You have a highly developed critical faculty and so are good at quality control.	You can become preoccupied with what is wrong or missing and consequently may not appreciate what is actually there.
You have the ability to be exact, to get the correct point. You have a clarity of focus and intention. You like to be precise.	You can become pedantic about what is right. You can get overly preoccupied with details and with getting everything right. You can become obsessive or compulsive.
You are altruistic and have an idealistic concern for people and causes beyond yourself.	You may not consider your own needs, wants, and feelings as important as what you think you *should* do.

Positive Core Value Tendencies	Distorted Core Characteristics
You desire, are committed to and take action to bring about a better world.	You have a tendency to interfere with or to intrude upon others' lives to make them better—for their own good.
You have strong feelings about and become intensely involved in whatever you value.	You can be overzealous. You can be unwilling to see another point of view. You have difficulty stepping back and being dispassionate.
You are conscientious, dedicated, persevering, reliable, hardworking, and industrious.	You can become over-responsible and a workaholic. You become tense and live your life under pressure with time running out to do all the good that must be done.
You are serious. You live your life with high intentions, ideals, and purpose.	You can take yourself and situations too seriously. You develop an inability to play and have fun.
You have an appreciation for fairness and justice.	You are prone to resentment since you tend to readily judge that life isn't fair.
You have a strong moral character. You try to live your life true to a higher good and a higher vision. You want to live a life of moral purity.	You can be moralistic and puritanical. You are tyrannized by your *shoulds*.

Objective Paradigm
Wholeness

Adaptive Cognitive Schema:

You understand perfection to be a *process*, as something you will always be on your way towards.

You trust the growth process in yourself and others. The universe is unfolding as it should.

You can appreciate the moment as it is. You enjoy yourself and others as dappled. You are right now just where you ought to be.

Virtue: *Serenity*

Adaptive Emotional Schema:

You are in touch with and are at ease with yourself. You are able to relax in the process of living. You experience the balance and harmony between opposites.

Distorting Paradigm
Perfection

Maladaptive Cognitive Schema:

You think of perfection in terms of a finished *product*, as something you should have achieved yesterday.

You set your own unreachable standards because you don't trust your natural unfolding and development.

You believe you need to improve upon the moment. The better is the enemy of the good. Instead of leaving yourself, or others, alone, you interrupt and interfere by trying to make it better.

Passion: *Anger*

Maladaptive Emotional Schema:

Anger can become an habitual emotional attitude for you. You are resentful because nothing meets your high standards and your expectations aren't fulfilled. You engage in all-or-nothing, black-and-white thinking. Either it's perfect or it's no good at all.

Area of Avoidance: *Anger*

You are uncomfortable being angry and find this feeling unacceptable even though it is a frequent reaction of yours. Good boys and girls should not be angry.

Defense Mechanism: *Reaction Formation*

To keep your angry impulses out of your awareness, you do the opposite of what you are inclined to do. For example, instead of confronting someone, you are nice to them; or instead of being sexual, you become puritannical.

How the Distortion of This Style Developed

- You were rewarded for being good and doing the right thing; you were punished for being bad and doing bad things.
- You got approval by being a good boy or good girl.
- You developed the belief that you were "somebody" if your ideals were higher than everybody else's, and you were "nobody" if you weren't perfect.
- You believed that by seeking excellence and having high standards you would be better than others.
- Being an over-achiever brought you good feelings and social approval.
- You came to believe that others wouldn't like you unless you were perfect.
- You discovered you could do things better or do things right if you did them yourself.
- You learned to control yourself and others and the situation by following the rules and prescribed *shoulds.*
- You were given, or you assumed, responsibility at a young age. You were expected to grow up early and be a parent to your siblings and maybe even to your own parents.
- You may have been the eldest or an older child.
- You learned at home or at school that being angry was unacceptable.

What You Miss as a Result of the Distortion of Your Style

- Spontaneity; fun; lighthearted gaiety.
- More carefree interactions with people.
- Trust in yourself, others, reality.
- Going with the flow; enjoying the process instead of controlling and pushing the river.
- Feeling relaxed.
- Tolerance and acceptance instead of being under the gun, scrutinized, criticized, pressured.
- Being yourself instead of having to prove yourself.
- Living the unexamined life.
- Doing something half-well just because you like to do it or because it's worth doing even half-well.

Paradigm Shifts You May Experience
Under Stressful Conditions

A Shift to the Low Side of Your Own Style

- You may try even harder to right the situation or make yourself better.
- You might strive more, push more, work more—to the point of exhaustion.
- You may become more rigid and strict with yourself and others.
- You may get more resentful because your goodness isn't fairly recompensed. You are good, you try hard, and you don't feel rewarded; and that isn't fair.
- You might become more serious, angry, frustrated, morose, and depressed.

A Shift to the Low Side of Style 4

- You may feel misunderstood, victimized, taken advantage of. You may feel bad because the world doesn't appreciate your efforts to make it better.
- You might attempt to be *special* if you can't be right or perfect enough.

- You may become more critical of yourself sometimes to the point of saying: *"What's the use. I'm hopeless. I'll never be good enough."*
- You may turn your anger on yourself and become depressed instead of channeling your energy into productive problem solving.
- You may give up on your precision and exactness and begin to exaggerate the situation and become overwhelmed by your feelings. You avoid ordinary experience and become dramatic.
- You may engage in *stinkin' thinkin'* by absolutizing and catastrophizing and by getting stuck in the polarities of either/or; black/white.
- Instead of taking action and doing something about what's wrong, you may become demoralized and immobilized. You may find yourself mired in melancholy and self-pity.
- You may get discouraged and give up on your ideals and goals.
- You may avoid looking at and dealing with reality in a straightforward, no-nonsense manner and become manipulative.

A Shift to the High Side of Style 4

- Here you get into your real feelings. You get in touch with your real preferences and identity and disidentify with your external and internal "shoulds" and expectations.
- You go in search of your real self instead of trying to realize your idealizations.

Paradigm Shifts You May Experience
Under Relaxed Conditions

A Shift to the High Side of Your Own Style

- You become forgiving of yourself and others.
- You accept yourself and the situation as it is instead of being critical and immediately wanting to change something. You let the weeds grow with the wheat. You accept yourself as dappled.

- You practice the Serenity Prayer and are more tolerant and patient.
- You shift your categories from either/or and all-or-nothing to both/and, continuum, process.
- You can ask yourself what you're angry about and check whether your expectations for yourself and others are unrealistically high.
- You express your anger cleanly or let it go instead of holding onto it and remaining resentful.
- You are more accepting of all your feelings—especially your sexual and aggressive responses. What you think are demons are actually *daimons* (friendly helpers).

A Shift to the High Side of Style 7

- You can say to yourself *"I'm okay even though I'm imperfect."*
- You take yourself and the situation less seriously. You get in touch with your playful side. You take a break before you break.
- You are more spontaneous. You let yourself go and let things happen instead of trying to get more control.
- You lighten up instead of getting more heavy and serious. You take your foot off the brake when you're skidding vs. pushing on the brake harder.
- You can go with the flow instead of against it. You don't push the river since it flows by itself. You trust the process. Everything, including you, is on the way.
- You can ask the child in you what she or he needs and wants.
- You can do what is desirable and pleasurable instead of what *should* be done.
- You use divergent vs. convergent thinking. There are many ways to solve a problem vs. only one right way. You are more creative and imaginative.
- You look at what's right in yourself and the situation instead of what's wrong. You can look at what's there vs. what isn't there. You can see the glass as half-full just as well as half-empty.

A Shift to the Low Side of Style 7

- You may try to escape the present pain or situation through addictions or other pleasurable trapdoors (e.g., you may try to avoid your inner voices and "shoulds" through addictions to alcohol, drugs, sex, etc.).

Style 2
The Loving
Person

Positive Descriptors of Your Style

helping
unselfish
giving
sensitive
complimenting
caring
loving
nurturing
gentle
sympathetic

affirming
accepting
sacrificing
other-centered
compassionate
listening
praising
serving
relationship-oriented
supporting

Negative Descriptors of Your Style

intrusive
interfering
possessive
manipulative
demanding
victim
rescuing
complaining
guilt-inducing
nonconfronting

unwilling to receive
overprotecting
martyr
other-directed
needy
smothering
infantilizing
undeserving of help
jealous
overly sweet

Positive Core Value Tendencies	Distorted Core Characteristics
You value and are attracted to *love*. You want to make the world a more loving place to live in.	You can overidentify with the *idealized self-image* of being *loving* and *helpful.* You are acceptable only if you are loving and nice.
You are naturally a giving, generous, helpful person. You enjoy giving to others. You are generous with yourself, time, energy, and possessions.	You can become a compulsive helper. You give love to gain attention and approval. You expect appreciation in return for your care.
You are supportive, nurturing, and considerate.	You can be overprotective and infantilize others and make them dependent on you.
You spontaneously appreciate, approve, applaud, and praise others' gifts.	You can manipulate others to like you by giving strokes to get strokes.
You have the ability to build people up and make them feel good about themselves.	You have difficulty expressing your negative feelings such as anger and disappointment and confronting things you don't like in others.
You are gentle and kindhearted and work toward establishing harmony and reconciliation.	It's hard for you to be assertive and/or angry. You can overdo trying to please others.
You have an intuitive sense for what others need, want, and are feeling.	You can be out of touch with your own needs, wants, and feelings.

Positive Core Value Tendencies	Distorted Core Characteristics
You are sociable, friendly, and approachable. Relationships are what life is all about for you.	You get anxious when you are alone. You may not know how to relate except through helping. Curiously enough, you may fear intimacy.
You enjoy helping others grow and supporting them.	It is difficult to leave others on their own, to let them grow up—or to let them fall down.
You are a good listener. You listen with your heart and are nonjudgmental.	You are prone to giving advice. You desire to control others by being helpful. You want to be important in someone's life because of all you've done for them.
Your sense of worth comes from yourself. You are filled with love from the inside out, like a wellspring.	Your worth comes from being needed and from others' approval. *"I am somebody if I'm needed."* Love comes from outside in to fill you.
If someone is hungry, you teach them how to fish so they can feed themselves.	If someone is hungry, you give them a fish so they will need to return to you to be fed.

Objective Paradigm
Freedom

Adaptive Cognitive Schema:

You understand freedom to mean living within the natural laws and limits of giving and receiving.

You are interdependent; it is more blessed to give *and* to receive.

You are responsive to the unfreedom in others. You are able to set others free.

Virtue: *Humility*

Adaptive Emotional Schema:

When you experience humility, you accept your own limits and boundaries. You are able to say *no* as well as *yes*. You are able to take time out for yourself.

Distorting Paradigm
Codependence

Maladaptive Cognitive Schema:

You believe freedom means being free from needs and being free from needing others' help.

You are codependent; it is more blessed to give *than* to receive.

You yourself are enslaved by caring for others to gain self-worth, and you bind others to you because they need you.

Passion: *Pride*

Maladaptive Emotional Schema:

You are proud when you believe you have unlimited resources to give. You believe you don't need or don't deserve help. You are liable to burn out.

Area of Avoidance: *Personal Needs*

You have difficulty getting in touch with and accepting your own needs. You are either not aware of them at all or else you don't want to burden others with your needs. You are afraid you can't be a helper and be needy at the same time.

Defense Mechanism: *Repression*

Because your own needs make you anxious, you keep them out of your awareness by repressing them. You project your needs onto others (so other people are needy, but you aren't).

How the Distortion of This Style Developed

- You got approval for helping and giving and not asking for much for yourself.
- You learned how to be sweet, funny, cute, and charming to get attention and to win affection.
- You received appreciation for your kindnesses.
- You became needed and important to people by helping them.
- You were made to feel guilty and to believe you were selfish if you expressed your own needs or cared for yourself.
- You discovered that to survive you needed to figure out what the other person wanted and then provide for their wants.
- You found that changing yourself to meet others' needs was preferable to remaining true to yourself and to your own needs.
- You had to provide emotional support for your parents—sometimes to the point of becoming the parent in your family.
- What *you* wanted or really needed wasn't empathized with or inquired about.
- You got rewarded for empathizing with others and making them feel better.
- You found that *moving toward* others in affection worked better for you than *moving against* others with anger or assertion or *moving away from* others by detaching yourself.

- You survived by being dependent on others' approval and by making yourself needed by them through your service.
- You experienced that pleasing others worked better than pleasing yourself.

What You Miss as a Result of the Distortion of Your Style

- The joy of receiving without having to earn what you have been given; the experience of grace.
- Letting others feel good by giving to you.
- A sense of worth based on who you are vs. what you can give.
- The inner freedom that comes from an inner sense of approval and security vs. seeking approval from the outside.
- The experience of intimacy in a reciprocal relationship.
- Being really known by someone else, including your needs and vulnerabilities.
- The experience of self-expression vs. self-renunciation or effacement.
- Freedom in relationships where you don't have to be in control through helping.

Paradigm Shifts You May Experience
Under Stressful Conditions

A Shift to the Low Side of Your Own Style

- You may increase your helping activity, still not get the appreciation you think you deserve, feel victimized and a martyr, and then reproach others for not caring for you more.
- You might try to get people to feel guilty to manipulate them to approve of you and appreciate you.
- As you approach burnout and exhaustion, you may become irritable, depressed, resent others' expectations, and wonder what it's all about.

A Shift to the Low Side of Style 8

- You may become vengeful and vindictive (at least in your fantasies) toward those who don't appreciate you enough.
- You may become a persecutor instead of a rescuer.
- You may lose touch with your natural gentleness, become tough and develop a hard shell to protect your vulnerable self-esteem.
- You may become bitter, jaded, and distrustful of others.
- You may cease helping others (for the time being) and tell them they're on their own.
- You may try to get others to be dependent on you so you can have power and control over them.
- Instead of asking for help, you may attempt to be more independent and refuse to need others. You may avoid not only your own needs, but any form of weakness.
- You may become less open to others and to yourself.

A Shift to the High Side of Style 8

- You may get in touch with your real inner power and be genuinely free of your need for others' approval and appreciation.
- You may establish stronger self boundaries, claim your own autonomy, stand on your own two feet, and not alter yourself to gain others' affirmation.
- You may take responsibility for your own needs and leave others responsible for their needs.
- You may express yourself honestly and forthrightly instead of trying to please others and say what you think they want to hear.

Paradigm Shifts You May Experience
Under Relaxed Conditions

A Shift to the High Side of Your Own Style

• You find sources for your self-worth in other places besides helping.

• You get in touch with your *own* needs, wants, and feelings.

• You give yourself permission to take time for yourself and take time alone for yourself.

• You develop a consistent self that doesn't alter to meet others' wishes and needs.

• You can negotiate with others as an equal. You are not only good at helping others express their needs but you can also make sure your own needs are represented and heard.

• You can ask others for help directly vs. indirectly through helping them. You can make straightforward demands on others for what is rightly due you.

• You exercise self-care. You do what you need to do for yourself. You deserve to care for yourself, and you deserve to be cared for.

• You take a realistic accounting of your assets and limitations and own both of them. This is what humility means for you.

• You say "no" when you mean "no" and "yes" when you mean "yes."

• You let others take care of themselves. You take responsibility for your needs and let others take responsibility for their needs.

• You give because you want to rather than because you need appreciation and approval in return.

• You let yourself receive from others. You can let others gift you.

A Shift to the High Side of Style 4

- You can say to yourself, "*I am special and so my needs are as important as anyone else's.*"
- You get in touch with culture and beauty.
- You develop your creative, self-expressive side (vs. being self-effacing). You can express your needs through creativity.
- You get in touch with your own unique identity and feelings and inner space. You get in touch with your sadness and regret over abandoning yourself in the service of others.

A Shift to the Low Side of Style 4

- You may take on a pretentious, artistic image instead of a genuine expressive spirit.
- You may become petulant and demand that others appreciate you and recognize your specialness.

Style 3
The Effective
Person

Positive Descriptors of Your Style

efficient	*popular*
successful	*active*
get things done	*dynamic*
motivator	*multi-faceted*
enthusiastic	*organized*
pragmatic	*self-assured*
practical	*marketer*
goal-oriented	*industrious*
energetic	*team-builder*
manager	*competent*

Negative Descriptors of Your Style

mechanical	*self-promoting*
get ahead	*appearances*
calculating	*jet set*
impatient	*success-driven*
expedient	*slick*
workaholic	*political*
chameleon-like	*misrepresenting*
scheming	*overachiever*
popularizer	*role-playing*
image-conscious	*ignore feelings*

Positive Core Value Tendencies	Distorted Core Characteristics
You are attracted to and value efficiency, productivity, industriousness, and competence.	You can overidentify with the *idealized self-image* of being *successful* and *productive* such that your worth depends on what you do instead of who you are.
You possess a natural organizational ability.	You can become overly efficient, machine-like, and ultra-programmed.
You have the ability to get things done.	You may substitute projects for persons.
You make a good salesperson. You exude confidence and competence and so people are willing to buy you and your product.	You can become a *marketing personality.* Your worth depends upon how well you can sell yourself or how marketable you are.
You make a good team person. As a team leader, you are able to organize, run, and motivate a team. As a team member, you can carry out your own responsibilities.	You can lose your personal identity by conforming to the group image or to the image of what the group wants you to be.
You are a good energizer. You have the energy to accomplish things and you are able to motivate others.	You always have to be on the go. You are unable to slow down or you're afraid to relax. You believe that *progress is our most important product.*

Positive Core Value Tendencies	Distorted Core Characteristics
You are friendly, gregarious, and sociable.	Your relationships can be utilitarian and superficial.
You have an intuitive sense for what people expect. You instinctively know what image to present to be successful.	You may sell out and lose your personal self for the sake of a public mask.
You are adaptable. You can negotiate and compromise to get things accomplished.	You can be chameleon-like. You may betray your inner self for the sake of a role and compromise.
You are optimistic, enthusiastic, and self-confident.	You may deceive yourself and others by only portraying a successful image.
You have the capacity for hard work. You have tremendous enthusiasm for projects and goals.	You can become a workaholic. You exhibit Type A behavior. You perform and achieve in order to get approval.

Objective Paradigm
Hope

Adaptive Cognitive Schema:

You can trust that all will run smoothly even when you're not working. You trust and have hope the world won't stop when you do.

You operate in harmony with natural life processes and within the social and natural laws.

Distorting Paradigm
Efficiency

Maladaptive Cognitive Schema:

You believe that the smooth running of the organization or operation or cosmos depends mainly on your interventions.

You believe you are above the law. Your own operating rules are more efficient than universal principles. You may come to believe that the end justifies the means.

Virtue: *Truthfulness*

Adaptive Emotional Schema:

You are truthful to your own inner self, feelings, and desires.

Your outer image matches your inner reality.

You are honest and loyal to others.

Passion: *Deceit*

Maladaptive Emotional Schema:

You lose touch with your real feelings and wants and present programmed, planned feelings instead.

You can deceive yourself and others into believing that the image presented is your real self. You live out of an image vs. out of real emotional preferences.

You show others what you think they want to see or what looks successful.

Area of Avoidance: *Failure*

The area you are out of touch with and avoid is failure. You want to present an image of success so you hide anything that may appear less than successful or you reframe happenings in your life (i.e., you say, "There are no failures in life; there are only learning experiences").

Defense Mechanism: *Identification*

To keep failure out of your awareness, you identify with whatever successful mask or role you are playing at the time. You identify with your role instead of with yourself.

How the Distortion of This Style Developed

- You were rewarded for your achievements rather than for yourself.
- Your worth depended on what you did instead of who you were.
- You were loved for what you produced or for the status you achieved.
- Playing a role was safer and got you further than being yourself.
- Performance and image were rewarded in place of emotional connections and deep involvements with others.
- You may have been a precocious child who got approval and attention by being successful at what you did, but you lost touch with your own feelings and preferences.
- Success, winning, getting ahead, and looking good were all emphasized in your family.
- Being the way other people wanted you to be got you what you wanted. You learned how to perform instead of how to be.
- Being efficient, organized, goal-oriented, and hard-working got you ahead of others.

- Programming yourself and being adaptable helped you to survive.

What You Miss as a Result of the Distortion of Your Style

- The security that comes from knowing your worth is based on your self instead of your productions.
- Knowing your value doesn't depend on market conditions, i.e., what others expect of you now.
- The experience of being appreciated for yourself and not for your achievements.
- Being yourself, expressing yourself, letting others know you without having to filter yourself through a role or mask.
- Not being afraid of failing; detachment from success; doing something because it's worth doing whether it's successful or not.
- Feeling your own feelings vs. replacing them with performance.
- Being the master of your work instead of being mastered by your work.
- The ability to relax and let others run things or let the universe run itself.
- Emotional involvement with others resulting from the meeting of two real selves; genuine intimate relationships.

Paradigm Shifts You May Experience
Under Stressful Conditions

A Shift to the Low Side of Your Own Style

- You may work harder, be even more on the go, take on more projects, shake more hands, put out even more press releases on yourself and your projects.
- You may become more concerned about your image and may imitate other roles or models instead of expressing yourself.
- You may doubt your self-worth and whether you really do have anything to contribute.

A Shift to the Low Side of Style 9

- Besides wanting to avoid failure, you may also try to avoid conflict, both inner conflict and conflict with others.
- Instead of dealing with the pain or the problem, you may avoid it, procrastinate, distract yourself, or numb yourself.
- You may replace or numb your real feelings with more work.
- You may give up on your natural efficiency and problem-solving abilities and say, "*What's the difference*" or "*What's the use, it doesn't matter.*"
- You may doubt yourself instead of trusting your genuine inner responses and desires.
- You may seek solutions from outside yourself vs. from within your own self and potentials.
- You may turn off your smooth running machine and go to bed. You go from on to off, from exertion to exhaustion.
- You may become resigned to how things are rather than trying to change them.
- You may turn to alcohol, drugs, eating, etc. if success and work don't seem fulfilling.
- You may become even more neglectful of your real self.

A Shift to the High Side of Style 9

- You slow down to allow your real feelings and preferences to arise.
- You become more introverted and reflective and let your inner self develop.
- You become more contemplative and receptive to balance your activity.
- You can be at one with another in a self-forgetting manner.
- You are more at peace with yourself and less driven.

Paradigm Shifts You May Experience
Under Relaxed Conditions

A *Shift to the High Side of Your Own Style*

- You save some energy for the development of your self instead of putting it all into your image or projects.
- You resist changing how you present yourself just to manipulate others.
- You are more honest. You discover your real feelings and tell the truth about them instead of exhibiting what you think you should feel in your role. You consider any lying to be a form of addiction.
- You accept failure as part of your life vs. blaming it on someone else or calling it something different (a learning experience, a partial success, etc.).
- You no longer act so mechanically and efficiently. You can drop out of the rat race.
- You can trust that the universe is running smoothly and on schedule and it can get along without you from time to time.
- You want to manifest and actualize what is real and worthwhile vs. the image that society rewards.
- You discover your lost child and develop the real you. You can separate yourself from your image.
- You want to work for society and the common good. You work for the benefit of others and not just to be successful.
- You allow yourself to get in touch with your physical sensations (i.e., fatigue).

A *Shift to the High Side of Style 6*

- You are loyal to yourself and others instead of to your products. *"To thine own self be true."*
- You are trustworthy as well as competent. This combination makes a good leader.
- If you believe in something, you stay with it even though it may not be socially applauded and popular. If it's worth doing, you do it even though you may fail.

- You can express doubts. You no longer have to be competent about everything.
- You cooperate with others vs. compete with them. You trust that others can get things done.

A Shift to the Low Side of Style 6

- You might become even more obedient and conforming to external expectations.
- You could become even more of a company man or woman.
- You might lose yourself in some authority figure or guru.
- You might experience fear and panic as you relax and come back to yourself.

Style 4
The Original
Person

Positive Descriptors of Your Style

sensitive
original
intense
making beautiful
involved
caring
good taste
distinctive
feeling
quality

classy
creative
refined
intuitive
nostalgic
aesthetic
cultured
expressive
questing

Negative Descriptors of Your Style

special
up and down
aloof
dramatic
exaggerating
possessive
complaining
precious
high-strung
clinging

snobbish
eccentric
mourning
controlling
attention-demanding
shifting emotions
standoffish
elite
overly-sensitive
misunderstood

Positive Core Value Tendencies	Distorted Core Characteristics
You are highly individual and value *originality*. You put your personal touch on everything you are involved in.	You can overidentify with the *idealized self-image* of being *special* and *unique*. You may become an eccentric caricature of originality.
Like a poet, you have an ability to make the ordinary extraordinary. You can take what is plain and make it special, like an oyster changes a grain of sand into a pearl.	You believe you must be unique, original, different; otherwise you are nobody. Your identity and worth depend on your being *special*.
You value and appreciate *beauty*. You want to make the world a more beautiful place. You have a highly developed aesthetic sense.	You can become an aesthete and artificially cultivate an artistic sensitivity. You can make a cult of art and beauty as an escape from mundane life.
You have an innate sense for quality. You have good taste and class.	You can look down on others for their philistine tastes. You may consider others to be tacky.
You are creative and imaginative. You favor creative channels of expression.	You believe you are so sensitive and your experience is so deep that mere words can't express it.
You are highly intuitive. You are in touch with your own and the collective unconscious.	You often feel misunderstood because no one experiences things as deeply as you do.

Positive Core Value Tendencies	Distorted Core Characteristics
Your self boundaries are fluid so you can empathize with and understand others' experiences.	Your self boundaries become too permeable such that you take on others' feelings and lose touch with your own feelings and sense of yourself.
You are highly attuned to the feelings, moods, tone, and spirit of the group.	You can become overwhelmed by your feelings and those of others and not be able to detach and step back from them.
You are sensitive toward the fragile feelings of hurt, pain, loss, and grief.	You are prone to melancholy. You believe your suffering makes you special.
You have a sense for the drama and tragedy of life.	You can overreact and dramatize. Drama creates excitement, dispels boredom, and helps create a sense of being special.
You have a strong emotional resonance and responsiveness to life.	Your intense emotions may frighten others away. *"I feel, therefore I am."*
You are romantic, poetic, nostalgic.	You may live in your romantic fantasies instead of in real life.
You feel fulfilled and whole in the present.	You focus on what is missing in the present; you can be nostalgic about paradise lost in the past and yearn for fulfillment in the future.

Objective Paradigm
Originality

Adaptive Cognitive Schema:

You are in touch with your real self and feel whole and complete. You believe you already are original.

You feel connected to yourself, to your roots and to the ground of your being. You feel at home.

Virtue: *Equanimity*

Adaptive Emotional Schema:

Right now you have everything you need to be perfectly happy. You appreciate yourself and your unique parcel of talents.

You express a balanced appropriate response to inner and outer stimuli.

Distorting Paradigm
Specialness

Maladaptive Cognitive Schema:

You feel sad because you have become separated from your essential nature. You feel incomplete, inauthentic, lacking, and disoriented. You believe you must do something to make yourself special.

You feel abandoned, left behind. You see yourself as an aristocrat in exile, apart from the main. If you make yourself special, then maybe others will remember you and love you.

Passion: *Envy*

Maladaptive Emotional Schema:

You envy others who seem to have something you're missing. You envy others' relationships and happiness and naturalness.

You have exaggerated, dramatic mood swings.

Area of Avoidance: *Ordinariness*

You fear the common and ordinary. If you're ordinary, you're nobody. The ordinary is boring and you want to be exciting. To exist you need to stand out from the crowd.

Defense Mechanism: *Introjection*

Instead of simply grieving, letting go of the past, and getting on with your life, you carry your suffering and loss around inside of you. This melancholy is a familiar companion, and it makes you feel special. Yearning and longing are constantly in the background of your experience.

How the Distortion of This Style Developed

- You originally felt close to a strong parent (often the father), then that parent went away (perhaps because your parent died, or your parents divorced, or the parent became busy at work, or a sibling was born, or the parent withdrew for some other emotional reason).
- You felt abandoned and interpreted that experience to mean there was something wrong with you or you weren't good enough—otherwise you wouldn't have been left behind.
- Then you tried to create yourself into a *special* person that the parent would notice and love. You came to believe that if you were special, then others would pay attention to you and wouldn't leave you.
- Your sense of tragedy, loss, and suffering may come from some original experience of being abandoned.
- Your mood swings may come from the alternation of a parent being available to you or not or of being kind or cruel. When the parent was there, you felt *good* about yourself and *up*. When the parent wasn't there, you felt *bad* about yourself and *down*.
- You felt expelled from the garden of love and are now longing to be readmitted.

- You received attention if you were sick or suffering; otherwise you weren't noticed.
- You got attention and your identity from living at the edges, at the extremes.
- You came to believe that being ordinary or calm meant being nobody or being boring.
- You felt alive especially when you made yourself *feel* intensely.
- Living intensely or living in your romantic world made you feel more special and important than living in the world as it is.
- You found you could compete successfully in the arena of style and flair.

What You Miss as a Result of the Distortion of Your Style

- The spontaneous expression of your thoughts and feelings.
- A balanced, modulated life style.
- Intimacy; being close to others without fear of rejection of being abandoned.
- The sense of fulfillment and satisfaction with who you are and what you have.
- The sense of being connected by your common humanity, being a part of the whole instead an island.
- Really having what you want vs. yearning for it.

Paradigm Shifts You May Experience
Under Stressful Conditions

A Shift to the Low Side of Your Own Style

- You may channel your feelings into your body and become physically ill instead of letting your feelings energize and guide your actions.
- Your mood swings may widen, with your lows becoming lower and your highs higher.
- Instead of being assertive and expressing your anger cleanly, you may become either passive-aggressive and suffer, complain and blame more, or you may become aggressive and vindictive and vengeful.

- As you feel worse about yourself or consider it's your fault that things aren't as you would like them, suicidal thoughts may preoccupy you more. Suicide may have several functions: it makes you special; it stops the suffering; it gets even with others; it lets them realize what they've done to you and how much they'll miss you.
- You may move away from people and isolate yourself more.
- You may throw yourself into work and become hyperactive to avoid dealing with your real issues.

A Shift to the Low Side of Style 2

- You may avoid dealing with your own needs and wishes and attend more to others' needs. Instead of being sensitive toward yourself, you become sensitive toward others.
- You might flee into service instead of healing yourself.
- You may repress your feelings instead of expressing them directly.
- You may become more manipulative instead of asking directly for what you want or taking action to get what you want.
- Your issues around dependence and independence may become exaggerated. You might become more possessive or more aloof.
- You may say, "*What's the use. I'm beyond repair, so I'll help others.*"
- You could become a suffering servant, a martyr, a sacrificial victim.

A Shift to the High Side of Style 2

- You can genuinely care for and serve people and get out of your self-absorption.
- You can accurately empathize with others.
- You can move towards others as well as away from them.

Paradigm Shifts You May Experience
Under Relaxed Conditions

A Shift to the High Side of Your Own Style

- You realize you are already *original.* You don't have to be eccentric or make yourself special. You search for and find the beloved within you vs. outside you.
- You can be spontaneous and let yourself go instead of being so composed.
- You can find the extraordinary in the ordinary.
- You accept your unique parcel of talents and don't compare yourself with others. You use your envy to help you locate and appreciate the values in others and to find those values in yourself.
- You pay attention to your real feelings vs. the exaggerated feelings that come from the excitement of your moods. You move from an addiction to romance and fantasy to action in real life.
- You stay in the here and now and realize that right now you have all you need to be happy.

A Shift to the High Side of Style 1

- You take an action-oriented, problem-centered approach. You think about what you can do about the problem vs. bemoaning your fate. You switch from a passive victim stance to being an active agent. You don't just yearn there, you do something. Put your show on the road instead of overrehearsing.
- You focus on one feeling at a time. What are you feeling now? And what do you want to do about it? You stay specific and resist generalizations and dramatizations. You stay with the facts.
- You maintain a sense of proportion, balance, equanimity. You don't exaggerate your response or heighten the stimuli. You do exactly what the situation requires. You do your work objectively.

- You can say, "*I am good*" or "*I'm good enough as I am*" instead of "*I'm not good enough.*" You reown your own strength, goodness, and wholeness.
- You can get in touch with your anger, focus it, and use it to get what you want instead of turning your anger against yourself, feeling depressed, and believing you don't deserve or can't attain what you want. You ask directly for what you want and state your needs directly.
- You realize that *realistic* isn't necessarily philistinistic.
- You can commit yourself to being in the world even though it is flawed and unfulfilling. You contribute to something you believe in.

A Shift to the Low Side of Style 1

- You may throw yourself into work and become hyperactive.
- You may get messianic about your fantasies and become emotionally overinvolved with your idealistic principles. "I *must* do my life's work!"
- You can become overly critical of your relationships.

Style 5
The Wise
Person

Positive Descriptors of Your Style

thoughtful
scholarly
reflective
truth-seeking
prudent
observant
witty
pithy
reasonable
logical

circumspect
clear
understanding
nonintrusive
philosophical
perceptive
cool
informed
analyzer/synthesizer

Negative Descriptors of Your Style

operate alone
miserly
overly-detached
unfeeling
uncaring
avoid commitment
cold
heady
postpone action
contemptuous

reclusive
abstract
intellectual
uncommunicative
greedy
hidden
hoarder
vicarious experience
holding back
fear of feelings

Positive Core Value Tendencies	Distorted Core Characteristics
You value and are attracted to *wisdom,* knowledge, understanding. For you, the *intellect* is a person's highest faculty. *"I think, therefore I am."*	You can overidentify with the *idealized self-image* of being *wise* and *perceptive.* You live too much out of your head and forget you also have feelings and a body.
Your passions are of the mind.	You can be overly intellectual. You may be afraid of and out of touch with your feelings.
You are a seeker of truth. You want to discover what really is.	You can become overly analytical and skeptical. Your questioning can interfere with your acting.
You are a perceptive, insightful, original thinker.	You may be unwilling to consider others' perceptions and ideas.
You have the ability to objectively and dispassionately observe.	You may stay in the observer position on the sidelines and not participate in life.
You are good at abstracting, synthesizing, and integrating different points of view and disparate elements.	You may not make a decision or act until you have the certitude that you have all the facts. You want to know everything before you do anything.
You are a fair, nonjudgmental witness.	You may be unwilling to disclose your own position.

Positive Core Value Tendencies	Distorted Core Characteristics
You are a good listener. You are gentle, patient, and non-threatening.	You may not contribute much to conversations. You let others do all the talking.
You have the ability to get to the essence or heart of the matter. You can peer through extraneous details to get to basic structures.	You can reduce life to bare dry bones (X-ray pictures) and miss the juicy, meaty aspects of life.
You can communicate in clean, clear, concise statements about what the issue really is.	You can be stingy with your communications. You speak in epigrams or one-liners and are unwilling to elaborate on what you've said.
You have an appreciation for solitude.	You can be addicted to privacy. You have an exaggerated need for space and anonymity.
You are independent and resourceful.	You can be a loner who wants to do everything out of your own resources.
You are reserved, respectful, and nonintrusive.	You have overdeveloped the tendency to *move away from* people. And it's difficult for you to move forward with either affection or assertion.

Objective Paradigm
Understanding/Transparency

Adaptive Cognitive Schema:

Your wisdom and understanding come from experience, participation, and involvement. You know with your body-feelings-mind.

You share your inner life to enrich the world. You freely give what you have freely received. You are generous with your self, feelings, ideas, and time.

Virtue: *Detachment*

Adaptive Emotional Schema:

You possess the spirit of non-attachment. You take what you need and let the rest go.

You express a balanced appropriate response to inner and outer stimuli.

Distorting Paradigm
Intellectualization/ Anonymity

Maladaptive Cognitive Schema:

Your knowledge comes too exclusively through your perceptions and watching and intellect. You know through your head or vicarious experience.

You desire anonymity, to hide and observe. You want to see but not be seen.

Passion: *Avarice*

Maladaptive Emotional Schema:

You are greedy. To avoid an inner sense of emptiness or feel externally dependent on others, you fill yourself and store up in yourself information and materials.

You hoard information and hold onto what you have and know. You are stingy with your time, possessions, ideas, feelings, and self.

Area of Avoidance: *Emptiness*

Since you repress your feelings and minimize your intimate interactions with others, you can experience a sense of inner emptiness. You may believe you have nothing to offer. You are searching for the meaning of life. You also fear being emptied by others and so withdraw and hold on tight.

Defense Mechanism: *Isolation*

To avoid feeling empty, you isolate yourself in your head away from your feelings and people. You go to your thoughts where you feel full and comfortable. You also isolate or compartmentalize one time or period of your life from the next.

How the Distortion of This Style Developed

- You may have experienced an early separation from your mother so an initial bonding with her didn't take place and you withdrew into yourself.
- You experienced your mother and/or father (and so the world) as being depriving and withholding. So you became depriving, too, both toward others and toward yourself.
- You may have experienced your parents as being too intrusive, so you withdrew to protect your boundaries.
- You may have felt overprotected, smothered, or engulfed, so you retreated into your mind or into books.
- You discovered that the best offense was a good defense.
- You found that being invisible was a good way to survive. It's hard to hit a target you can't see.
- You can't be blamed for what you never said. If people don't know what you're thinking, they can't criticize you.
- You didn't feel listened to, so you didn't speak unless you were sure people wanted to hear you.
- You were successful with academics and were rewarded for being studious.
- Your inner world became safer, more secure, more controllable and more interesting than the outer world.

- The expression of feelings—especially anger or any exuberant feelings—were not encouraged in your family.

What You Miss as a Result of the Distortion of Your Style

- The delights of being a sensual, bodily person.
- The joy and fulfillment of giving.
- The meaning that comes from becoming involved and engaged with life.
- The deep satisfactions of intimate, mutual personal relationships.
- The fun and excitement of being in the game instead of keeping yourself on the sidelines.
- The experience of being a part of (vs. apart from) humanity; feeling connected, belonging.
- The experience of trust and cooperation instead of trying to do everything yourself.
- The energy and aliveness and power of your own emotions which are your allies, not your enemies.
- Self-confidence.

Paradigm Shifts You May Experience Under Stressful Conditions

A Shift to the Low Side of Your Own Style

- Instead of moving out to make contact with people, either through assertion or affection, you may withdraw further and fall more silent.
- You might feel more inadequate and think you are unable to influence the situation, so you may do nothing.
- You may repress your feelings more or channel them into fantasies instead of into behavior.
- You may *back up* more and move *up* into your control tower in your head instead of moving *down* to get grounded in your feelings and body and then moving *out* into interactions.
- Instead of expressing your needs and negotiating, you take your ball and bat and go home and refuse to play in the game, believing that the world is non-negotiable.

- You may hold in your anger and become cold—like dry ice. You may freeze people out instead of engaging with them or inviting them in.
- You may become contemptuous of others instead of interacting with them. You may become critical and cynical as ways of avoiding contact.
- You may unplug, disconnect, and feel more alienated and isolated.

A Shift to the Low Side of Style 7

- You may get more into your head, intellectualize, systematize, and spiritualize to avoid taking action.
- You may turn to humor to lighten the situation and make it seem less important to avoid asserting yourself.
- You might let your fear of suffering or getting hurt prompt you to avoid them by retreating.
- You might get into planning what you'll do the next time instead of doing something this time.
- You might look for what is good in the situation so you won't have to voice your displeasure at what you don't like.
- You may give up on your ability to analyze and go in depth into the matter at hand. Instead you may distract yourself with superficial diversions or pursue many interests at once rather than completing any one. You might become flighty and undependable.

A Shift to the High Side of Style 7

- Your imagination and visualizing capabilities may be enhanced.
- You can use your humor to help you move toward people and be more sociable and friendly.
- You are more spontaneous and use play as a way of taking the edge off social encounters.

Paradigm Shifts You May Experience
Under Relaxed Conditions

A Shift to the High Side of Your Own Style

- You own your relational powers. You *move toward*, protect, enrich, and enlarge others instead of defending yourself from others or holding back from them.
- You empathize as well as analyze; you listen with your heart as well as your head. You apply your knowledge instead of keeping it to yourself.
- You get in touch with your feelings, especially hurt and anger. You let them energize and express your real self.
- You allow yourself to be transparent. You come out in the open instead of trying to be invisible. You let yourself be known and seen. You challenge and let go of your addiction to isolation and privacy.
- You can successfully challenge your fear of looking foolish and your fear of making a mistake. You don't let them stop you from doing what you want. You don't have to know everything before you choose and act.
- You can come to each person and situation empty, without preconceptions, categories, and structures. You are open to what is there and trust your spontaneous response. You trust your inner perceptions, intuitions, and feelings.
- You stay with your sense of emptiness instead of trying to avoid it or fill it. You may discover it is really a fertile void, a container that is always open to the here and now.

A Shift to the High Side of Style 8

- You are in touch with your personal power. You *can* change and influence the situation. You do have something to offer. You are in touch with your inner authority and stand up for what you believe in. You can say to yourself, *"I am powerful; I can do."*

- You can own your assertive powers. You can *move against.* You can say what you want or don't want. You can ask for what you need. You balance input with output. You reach out vs. pull back.
- You consult your body, instincts, heart, and feelings as well as your head. You are in touch with your instinctual energy.
- You move "down and out" vs. "up and away": *down* into your feelings and gut reactions and *out* into action; instead of *up* into your thoughts and *away* from the situation. You put yourself out in the world.
- You use your power and assertion to establish and maintain stronger boundaries. You can set limits instead of retreating. You stay in the ring and don't jump out at the first sign of pain or opposition.

A Shift to the Low Side of Style 8

- You may become aggressive instead of assertive. You may become mean and cruel and use your power to grasp, hold on and remain stingy instead of being magnanimous and generous.
- You may exaggerate your independence and isolation and become more anti-social.
- You may become vindictive with a dose of paranoid thinking.

Style 6
The Loyal
Person

Positive Descriptors of Your Style

cautious
reliable
traditional
God-fearing
respectful
loyal
responsible
trustworthy
sensible
determined

prepared
conscientious
stabilizing
charming
prudent
honorable
tenacious
devil's advocate
authority conscious

Negative Descriptors of Your Style

dogmatic
suspecting
rigid
uptight
catastrophizing
authoritarian
phobic/counterphobic
timid
assume worst
indecisive

wary
conservative
vigilante
rule-follower or challenger
anxious
status quo
worrier
uncertain
need for guidelines
security conscious

Positive Core Value Tendencies	Distorted Core Characteristics
You are attracted to and value *loyalty*. You honor your commitments.	You can overidentify with the *idealized self-image* of being *loyal* and *doing your duty*.
When you give your word, you keep it. If you say you'll do something, you do it.	You can become rigid and inflexible. It may be difficult for you to change or reconsider your loyalties.
You are faithful to relationships. You make a gracious host or hostess. You are protective of those in your care. You are loyal and dedicated to your cause and group.	You can polarize reality and your relationships into friend or foe, in or out, for me or against me. While you are accepting of those inside the fold, you can become a persecutor of those outside the fold.
You are able to foster, support, and parent others.	You can become overprotecting, smothering, and restricting.
You make a devoted follower or leader. You are responsible and can be counted on to do what you're told or what you promise.	You may become authoritarian or anti-authoritarian. Your faith and devotion may be given blindly or attached to the wrong ideal.
You have a balanced attitude toward external authority and you trust your own inner authority.	You can be either overly fearful and dependent on authorities or overly challenge them to test whether they deserve their authority and your allegiance.

Positive Core Value Tendencies	Distorted Core Characteristics
You have respect for law and order.	You may exaggerate your appreciation for structure and order into a paranoid police state.
You have an appreciation for your heritage. You honor your past.	You can become ultraconservative. You may be fearful of and uncomfortable with anything new.
You are prudent and cautious.	You may be overly cautious and spread fear and alarm. *"Be careful or you'll get hurt."*
You have a sense of propriety. You are respectful and reverent towards others.	You can be stuffy, serious, and obsequious. You restrict your spontaneity.
You are cooperative.	You may be either excessively compliant or rebellious.
You are *semper fidelis*, always faithful and constant.	You can be super-orthodox and conservative.
You are *semper paratus*, always prepared and ready for a crisis.	You are wary, fearful, and worrisome. You have nothing to fear but fear itself.
You can be an adventurous explorer.	You may believe you need to prove yourself by your daring or your duty.

Objective Paradigm
Faith

Adaptive Cognitive Schema:

You have faith in a balanced and trustworthy world. You believe the universe is out to do you good, not to do you in.

You believe you are already connected to, trusted by, and on the side of the ground of your being. You believe the force is with you.

You are in touch with your own essence, spirit, and authority and with others' genuine selves which puts you at ease.

Virtue: *Courage*

Adaptive Emotional Schema:

Your strength comes from being in harmony with your inner self and with the objective laws of the universe.

You are naturally courageous when you need to be. You spontaneously respond well in crises.

Distorting Paradigm
Doubt/Dogma

Maladaptive Cognitive Schema:

You perceive the world as alien, hostile, threatening, and dangerous, and this gives rise to fear and suspicion in you.

You believe the force is against you, or at least is testing you to see whether you'll be faithful and acceptable. You automatically give your allegiance to authority or you doubt authority and yourself.

You are in touch with your own and others' inner judge and critic which makes you nervous and fearful.

Passion: *Fear*

Maladaptive Emotional Schema:

Fear puts you out of touch with your real self and the real world and so you need to create a substitute strength and bravado.

You may become *counterphobic* by recklessly pushing through your fears and forcing yourself to do what you're afraid of, or *phobic* by dying a thousand deaths through your cowardice and worry.

You are motivated by your heart and what you genuinely believe in.

You are driven by fear and doubt.

Area of Avoidance: *Deviance*

If you are fearful, you seek to be loyal and obedient, you consider any disobedience, rebelliousness, or following your own inner authority to be deviant, unlawful, and unacceptable.

If you are counter-fearful, you become rebellious and seek to challenge, evade, or escape from authority.

Defense Mechanism: *Projection*

You project onto others your own sense of disobedience and rebellion. *Other people* are trying to get away with things, and you need to monitor their activities and bring them in line with your authority's principles, or others are trying to trip you up and trap you.

How the Distortion of This Style Developed

- Your parents may have been authoritarian. They laid down the rules and you had to follow them.
- You had to please your parents and do what you were told vs. paying attention to what you wanted or thought or felt.
- Your parents may have been overly protective. They had a fearful attitude toward life which you picked up.
- You learned that the world was a dangerous place to be guarded against.
- There may have been some family secret that needed to be kept inside the family. So boundaries were established between

inside and outside. Familial bonds and loyalty arose against the outside world.

- You found security in being close to authority.
- You decided to rebel against authority as a way to survive since the people who were authorities in your life abused their authority and couldn't be trusted.
- You came to believe that if you kept the law, the law would keep you.
- You got approval for being responsible, obedient, and hard-working.
- You had to assume the role of an adult before you were ready. You became the family caretaker.
- You felt incompetent because you weren't ready for this adult role and so you began to doubt yourself.
- Or you experienced a parent as being incompetent, and so you began to doubt authority.

What You Miss as a Result of the Distortion of Your Style

- A sense of inner security.
- Being able to do what you want vs. what you ought.
- A relaxed attitude toward yourself, others, life, and a higher power.
- A gracious approach to life.
- Being carefree.
- Being inner-directed instead of outer-directed.
- Trust in yourself and others.
- The freedom of the children of God: freedom from the law vs. enslavement and idolatry toward it; the law is for you and not vice versa.

Paradigm Shifts You May Experience Under Stressful Conditions

A Shift to the Low Side of Your Own Style

- You may become more indecisive and worrisome.
- As you become more fearful, you may worry more about

whether you're brave enough to do what is required of you. You may believe you need to prove yourself even more.

- You may become more suspicious of others.
- You might become more dogmatic and set in your beliefs and become more intolerant of other points of view.
- You might trust your inner authority less.
- You may act out against authority, becoming more rebellious and belligerent.

A Shift to the Low Side of Style 3

- Instead of relaxing, you may speed up and become busier.
- Instead of dealing with your inner issues, you might distract yourself with external matters and take on more projects.
- Not only might you run around in circles in your head by obsessing and worrying, but you may engage your gears and literally run around in circles in frantic activity to avoid dealing with your inner issues or to prove yourself and gain authority's or others' approval.
- You may try to substitute some external role for the inner security you're really seeking.
- You may start to deceive yourself and others about who you really are, what you really think and feel, and what you really want.
- You may want to avoid any semblance of rebellion or independent thought. And you may also begin to avoid any form of failure. As a result, your inner and outer freedom will become less and less.
- You may try to please authority and win them over by working hard, being faithful, doing what you're told, playing your part, etc.

A Shift to the High Side of Style 3

- You get in touch with your capacity to take action. You feel better when you are in action.
- You connect with your own competence and mastery to become proactive vs. reactive.

- You can channel your energy into goals and concrete plans instead of into fears and worst-case scenarios. You focus on what you can do vs. on what might go wrong.

Paradigm Shifts You May Experience
Under Relaxed Conditions

A Shift to the High Side of Your Own Style

- You trust your own instincts, viewpoints and inner authority. You become more autonomous vs. being dependent on others' opinions, especially authority's pronouncements. You are secure within yourself instead of seeking security from outside yourself. You develop a realistic belief in yourself and your abilities. You can affirm yourself.
- You develop the courage to be. You accept responsibility for your choices and act bravely. You trust your inner compass and desires. You believe that what you really want is what God wants for you.
- You trust that others aren't trying to get away with something. You believe they're trying to do the best they can. You don't project hostile intentions onto others.
- You recognize that rules are there for your benefit. You don't have to be a slave to them. You now follow the spirit of the law vs. the letter.
- You realize you are already a part of the operation or organization. You are already in the game. So you don't have to prove yourself to get in, and you don't have to worry about being thrown out.
- You can consider the positive outcomes as well as the negative ones. Your old inclination was to consider what could go wrong and that stopped you from acting. You were your own worst enemy. Now you can think of what might go right to motivate yourself to act.
- You trust your instinctual ability to protect and preserve yourself and those you love. You realize that nothing can harm your essence. You can challenge your fears—are they realistic or mythical?

A Shift to the High Side of Style 9

- You practice self-soothing and calming. You can say to yourself, "*I am settled*" vs. "*I am upset.*"
- You can be still and quiet. You realize the solution lies within you. You calm your waters and let the solution surface.
- Instead of making mountains out of molehills, you make molehills out of mountains. You can say, "*What's the big deal*" instead of making a big deal out of everything.
- You have the relaxed mind set, "*So what if I do this or think that*" vs. the fearful and indecisive mind set of "*What if I do this or that?*" You can go with the flow and trust the process.
- You can relax and float and let the stream support you. You realize that struggling is not the solution.
- You can find the truth in all sides of an issue instead of polarizing the issue and making one side all true and the other side all false.

A Shift to the Low Side of Style 9

- You may become even more doubtful, ruminating, and indecisive.
- You may find yourself procrastinating and doing unimportant things to distract yourself from doing what you really need to do. You may find it hard to prioritize and discern what you really want.
- You may numb yourself out or put yourself into some routine to avoid anxiety-provoking situations.

Style 7
The Joyful
Person

Positive Descriptors of Your Style

lighthearted
optimistic
friendly
enthusiastic
creative
visionary
gregarious
imaginative
joyful
merrymaking

extroverted
excitable
appreciative
fun-loving
funny
entertaining
lively
planning
bright
spontaneous

Negative Descriptors of Your Style

superficial
loquacious
narcissistic
cosmic
spacey
distracted
indulgent
light-headed
impulsive
irresponsible

inconsistent
unreliable
daydreamer
spotlight-grabbing
sybaritic
scattered
unrealistic
escapist
naive
dabbler

Positive Core Value Tendencies	Distorted Core Characteristics
For you the purpose of life is to *enjoy* it. You value *joy*. There is a delight, sparkle, and *joie de vivre* about you.	You can overidentify with the *idealized self-image* of being *okay.* You can overdo the pleasure principle and become overly attached to pleasure.
You are a celebrator of life.	You can become addicted to highs.
You have a great appreciation for life. Everything is recognized as gift.	You may not be willing to endure hard labor to get what you want.
You have a childlike responsiveness to the world. You are in touch with the immediacy of things.	You may be unwilling to follow up your initial enthusiasm with the boring work necessary to realize the project. The seed sprang up immediately but withered away because it didn't put down roots.
You are an advocate of growth, hope, and resurrection now.	You may trust only excitement, fireworks, consolation, and joy, and forget that growth also takes place in cold, dark silence.
You have an optimistic outlook on life. You can find the silver lining in black clouds. *"Two prisoners looked out from prison bars; one saw mud, the other saw stars."*	Your computer is set on *nice* and nothing is allowed in that is not nice. You can be a compulsive optimist seeing the world through rose-colored glasses.

Positive Core Value Tendencies	Distorted Core Characteristics
You have a creative imagination and are a wellspring of new ideas.	You may confuse your map and plan with reality and action.
You are lively, vivacious, and colorful.	You may be unwilling to look at the dark side of pain and suffering.
You are friendly and gregarious and are good at cheering people up.	Your relationships may remain superficial. *"Hale fellow well met."*
You are a natural entertainer and storyteller.	You may live your stories instead of your life.
You are a visionary, a long-range planner.	You can get into head trips instead of doing serious work.
You can generate endless possibilities. You are an intuitive person.	You can become a dilettante and jump from one interest to another without digesting anything thoroughly or without completing any project.

Objective Paradigm
Work

Adaptive Cognitive Schema:

When you are living in touch with your real self, then you are also living in accordance with the cosmic plan or the divine scheme of things. You understand that each person has a part to play in the evolution of humankind.

Work can be play when you do what you love doing.

Virtue: *Sobriety*

Adaptive Emotional Schema:

Sobriety means living in the present and living a balanced life, taking in only as much as you need and expending only as much energy as is called for.

Distorting Paradigm
Pleasure/Planning

Maladaptive Cognitive Schema:

When you lose touch with your real self and live out of your personality, then you are not participating in the larger scheme of things. You substitute your own plans and search for pleasure in place of deeper satisfactions.

If it isn't fun, it isn't worth doing and you don't stay with it for long.

Passion: *Gluttony*

Maladaptive Emotional Schema:

Gluttony means overindulgence, planning future fun-filled events, and spicing up life with excitement and fluff.

Area of Avoidance: *Pain and Suffering*

Since you want to appear happy and okay, you are uncomfortable with and find unacceptable any form of pain. You may either be out of touch with the pain in your life, or you are aware of it but are unwilling to show it to others since your job is to cheer people up, not weigh them down with your problems.

Defense Mechanism: *Sublimation*

To keep pain out of your awareness, you sublimate it and turn it into something interesting or good. You automatically look for the good in everything. So you might celebrate the new life of a deceased loved one rather than mourn their loss.

How the Distortion of This Style Developed

- You found that a cheerful, pleasant disposition earned approval from others and got you what you needed.
- You learned that your smiles elicited smiles from others.
- You were rewarded for cheering up the family, not complaining, and for keeping things light.
- Entertaining others and being the life of the party got you attention.
- People may have listened to your stories more than to your real self, or they were more interested in your stories than in your hurt or pain.
- You got more enjoyment from planning projects than from executing them.
- Your childhood was basically a happy one, or at least you turned it into being happy or you remember it as being happy.
- Even if you experienced adversity in your childhood, you learned to laugh about it to survive.
- You may have been shielded from hurt and pain or didn't experience much of either. And so you didn't learn how to deal with them—except by avoiding them.

- You may have learned that what you don't see won't hurt you.

What You Miss as a Result of the Distortion of Your Style

- A sense of inner strength and satisfaction that comes from working hard at something and accomplishing it.
- A deep character that is etched by perseverance and suffering and endurance.
- Experiencing the full range of emotions, the negative as well as the positive.
- Meeting your *Shadow* and discovering its riches.
- The tranquility of solitude, silence, and inner stillness.
- The experience of growth in desolation.
- Not being afraid of the dark.
- Thoroughly understanding something.
- Deep interpersonal relationships based on sharing all of yourself, not just the bright or light sides.

Paradigm Shifts You May Experience
Under Stressful Conditions

A Shift to the Low Side of Your Own Style

- You may get more into your head. You may intellectualize, spiritualize, and sublimate more.
- You may get more into planning and further away from doing. You may avoid doing hard work in favor of making future plans.
- You might try to avoid the present pain by imagining future or past pleasures.
- You may attempt to lighten things up even more, laugh off the situation, and not take yourself seriously.
- You may continue attempting to outrun your fears by looking for more parades to lead or join.

A Shift to the Low Side of Style 1

- You may become angry and resentful that your life is not as enjoyable as you would like it to be. Your joyful expectations are not being met.
- You may express your anger through sarcastic wit or critical remarks or through resentment and believing that life isn't fair—or at least not fun enough.
- You may complain and blame others for raining on your parade, spoiling your fun, popping your balloons. Others are keeping you from realizing all your fantastic schemes.
- You may give up on your natural appreciation for life and your spontaneous ability to find good in everything and begin to become critical and caustic toward yourself and others. You begin to notice what is missing instead of what is there.
- If you get too critical or too disappointed, you may become depressed.
- You may swing from being optimistic to being pessimistic, but probably not for long.
- You may give up trying to look okay. You may stop smiling.
- You may avoid and deny your anger as well as avoiding pain and suffering.

A Shift to the High Side of Style 1

- You can become more disciplined and focused and follow through on your plans and projects, bringing them to completion.
- Instead of doing what is pleasurable, you can be motivated by what is the right thing to do or what is called for.
- You take a more objective delineated point of view in place of a fantastic impressionistic vision.
- You attend to details and sweat the small stuff vs. going cosmic with global impressions.

Paradigm Shifts You May Experience
Under Relaxed Conditions

A Shift to the High Side of Your Own Style

- You can be present to all that is there: the good *and* the bad, the pleasurable *and* the painful, the light *and* the dark, the yin *and* the yang. Truth involves honoring both polarities.
- You can be sober. You aren't afraid to take yourself and the situation seriously. Even if you do get heavy, you know you won't crash.
- You trust that if you let go of your wings and balloons, you won't fall into the tomb. And even if you do, you believe that desolation and darkness can be growth-producing.
- You do what is worth doing. You realize happiness is contingent upon your doing your share of social and personal work.
- You can stay in the here and now and resist projecting yourself into the future. You do what you're doing instead of making future plans.
- You believe that your insights are important enough to work towards actualizing them.
- You stay with the pain instead of trying to avoid it, rationalize it, sublimate it, etc.
- Instead of making light of a situation, you can express your anger or be assertive.

A Shift to the High Side of Style 5

- You can say to yourself, "*I am wise and perceptive*" vs. "*I am a lightweight or scatterbrained.*"
- You can channel your energies and stay focused instead of scattering and getting distracted.
- You stay with what you're doing and thoroughly investigate it until you really understand it.
- You chew and digest instead of gulping down indiscriminately.
- You put your creative bursts and intuitions into some system and structure. You are thorough and methodical. This helps you take the next step of action.

- You learn to appreciate silence and aloneness.
- You can be still and observant. You can take the position of the fair witness, the detached observer.
- You watch vs. react. You develop your interiority.
- You practice detachment. You can move back a little from what's going on instead of losing yourself in what's happening.

A Shift to the Low Side of Style 5

- You may withdraw and try to disappear.
- You may compound your gluttonous life style with being avaricious and desirous of accumulating even more possessions and experiences.
- You might become more unhinged from reality and more glued to your fantasies and ideas.

Style 8
The Powerful
Person

Positive Descriptors of Your Style

forceful

strong

direct

assertive

.own person

autonomous

influential

hardworking

high energy

confident

magnanimous

strong-willed

no nonsense

take lead

fair

just

honorable

fearless

assured

competent

Negative Descriptors of Your Style

vengeful

unrefined

macho

bravuro

get even

possessive

overwhelming

intimidating

loud

gruff

bully

insensitive

non-listening

calloused

tough

domineering

belligerent

dictatorial

chip-on-shoulder

confrontive

Positive Core Value Tendencies	Distorted Core Characteristic
You are attracted to and appreciate *power.* You know how to get it, keep it, and use it.	You can overidentify with the *idealized self-image* of being *powerful* and *capable.* You can become addicted to power and control and rely on it to manipulate others.
You use your influence to bring about good.	You use your power to protect yourself instead of to help others.
You make a strong leader like a matriarch or a patriarch.	You can become a dictator, bully, godfather or godmother.
You are self-confident, self-assured and have a healthy self-image.	Your presence can be overbearing and intimidating.
You are independent and autonomous. You value being your own person.	You can exhibit an exaggerated independence and take pride in doing your own thing.
You can be magnanimous and use your personal power to contribute to and build up the community.	You can be self-aggrandizing and use your power against the community.
You have the ability to inspire others to accomplish great things.	You can coerce others by making them an offer they can't refuse. You influence by intimidation.
You are direct, straightforward, honest, and tell it like it is.	You can be overly blunt and crude.

Positive Core Value Tendencies	Distorted Core Characteristic
You can be a charismatic and inspiring person.	You can be insensitive to others' defenses and vulnerabilities in your unmasking of their pretensions.
You are able to cut through phoniness and fluff to get to the real issue. You believe in "no bullshit."	You may run roughshod over others or alienate them by taking over.
You are energized by challenge. You can take charge in difficult situations.	You can be aggressive. You get heard because you yell the loudest.
You are assertive and know how to get what you want.	You are often the topdog and can oppress others.
You have a concern for the underdog and will fight on his/her behalf.	You can intimidate and mesmerize others into following you.
You do everything with gusto, enthusiasm, and great energy.	You can be driven and use up people and things in your path.

Objective Paradigm *Justice*	Distorting Paradigm *Vindication*
Adaptive Cognitive Schema:	**Maladaptive Cognitive Schema:**
You have an appreciation for justice and equity. You believe in the equal distribution of power.	You believe in "an eye for an eye and a tooth for a tooth." Justice becomes vengeance, getting even to maintain the balance of power.
You trust the fairness of the universe. You believe that what goes around, comes around. " *Vengeance is mine, saith the Lord.* "	You judge that what is happening isn't fair. So you need to create your own truth and take justice into your own hands. *"Vengeance is mine, saith the Eight."*

Virtue: *Innocence*	Passion: *Lust*
Adaptive Emotional Schema:	**Maladaptive Emotional Schema:**
You possess a childlike innocence. You are capable of experiencing each moment fresh without expectations and prejudgments.	You come to each situation jaded, expecting trouble, or to be taken advantage of. You are therefore ready for a fight.
Innocence means not harming. You have the attitude, *"Why should I want to harm anyone and why would anyone want to harm me?"*	You have experienced aggression towards you in the past. So you want to get them before they get you.
You are satisfied with life as it is.	You are lustful, meaning you do everything to *excess.* You can be possessive, grabby, and demanding.

Area of Avoidance: *Weakness*

Since you want to appear strong, you must avoid any semblance of weakness. You are out of touch with your feminine side. You avoid tenderness, compassion, kindness, etc. as unbefitting a powerful person.

Defense Mechanism: *Denial*

To prevent weakness from showing up in your awareness or persona, you deny any presence of it. *"I don't hurt, I'm not nice, I'm not sentimental, I don't need you,"* etc.

How the Distortion of This Style Developed

- You may have been abused as a child and so became tough and aggressive in order to protect yourself.
- You may have witnessed considerable fighting and aggression in your family.
- You had to grow up fast and be hard to take care of yourself.
- You learned that when you challenged others or bullied them, you got your way.
- You were instructed to fight back and not put up with insults or injustices.
- You may have learned that in your family you don't get mad, you get even.
- You may have felt yourself to be a victim of injustice, so you grew up blaming the world.
- You learned never to give a sucker an even break.
- You learned never to show weakness if you wanted to survive.
- Since the world seemed to be arbitrary or unjust, you learned to make and follow your own rules.
- You realized you had a lot of energy and forcefulness. You had the ability to take charge, and you enjoyed being powerful.
- If a situation seemed threatening or falling apart, you felt more secure when you took control.

What You Miss as a Result of the Distortion of Your Style

- Being comforted by others and being touched by their care.
- Having someone speak up for you.
- Experiencing your own tenderness and softness and gentleness.
- Forgiveness and compassion.
- Being able to live with weakness instead of always having to deny it.
- The experience of reverence and respect for creatures instead of using them up.
- Letting your guard down and being vulnerable.
- The capacity to relax, to be present.
- Experiencing others' goodness and goodwill instead of anticipating their affronts.

Paradigm Shifts You May Experience Under Stressful Conditions

A Shift to the Low Side of Your Own Style

- You might try to take care of yourself by becoming more aggressive and tough. You send your anger out first to cover the hurt or sadness or disappointment you may really be feeling.
- You may become more intense, grabby, lustful, and possessive to fill up feeling empty inside.
- You may attempt to take more control and assume more power to feel secure.

A Shift to the Low Side of Style 5

- You may give up on your own power and withdraw. You may *move away from* people instead of *toward* them.
- You may become quiet and want to be by yourself. You may isolate yourself from others.
- You may turn your power against yourself and beat up on yourself for your perceived weaknesses and injustices.
- Instead of exploding, you *implode* your energy and suck it inside yourself.

- As a result of imploding, you might experience exaggerated feelings of deadness and emptiness.
- You may drive yourself into a black hole. Then you may either become suicidal or become more desperate in your attempts to avoid this inner emptiness through living intensely.
- You may break contact with others vs. making contact.
- You won't let others support you or comfort you.
- You may exaggerate being independent and on your own. You become the Lone Ranger or Rangerette.
- You might become overly heady and rational and use your intellect to defend yourself, blame others, or plot revenge.
- You may feel inadequate and unable to influence the situation.
- You may begin to distrust your instincts.
- You might move toward thinking and observing instead of doing.

A Shift to the High Side of Style 5

- You think before you act. You can think it out before you impulsively act it out.
- You can think clearly and dispassionately vs. with prejudiced preconceptions and caricatures.
- You connect your head and gut and heart and are genuinely present, spontaneous and compassionate vs. being internally disconnected and then feeling isolated, violent, or punishing.
- You appreciate and pursue knowledge for its own sake vs. as a way of having power over others.

Paradigm Shifts You May Experience
Under Relaxed Conditions

A Shift to the High Side of Your Own Style

• You let others speak up for you instead of always speaking up for them.
• You can share your vulnerable underside with others. You let them know your scared little kid. You let others support you.
• You move towards *interdependence* in place of your extreme self-sufficiency and fear of dependence.
• You trust others' motivations instead of challenging them and attempting to unmask their hidden motivations and intentions.
• You respect others' rights as much as you demand respect for your own.
• You speak the truth in a way that others can take it in instead of shoving it down their throat.
• You assume an attitude of innocence: why would anyone want to hurt you? And why would you want to hurt anyone?
• You come to each moment and situation fresh, without expectation of being hurt or taken advantage of and without memories of past wrongs and insults. You come with hands open vs. fists clenched.
• You trust that justice and fairness will come about without your intervention or having to get even. You realize it is not solely up to you to bring about justice and equity.

A Shift to the High Side of Style 2

• You can be compassionate toward yourself and others. You temper your justice with mercy.
• You can say, "*I am helpful; I am giving.*" You are giving instead of grabby.
• You use your power to build others up and empower them vs. tearing them down.
• You are empathic and sensitive toward your own needs and towards others' needs and feelings.
• You are in touch with your gentle side and tenderness. There

is nothing stronger than true gentleness and nothing gentler than true strength. You become soft vs. hard—tender vs. tough.
- You move *toward* others vs. *against* them. You resist moving toward violence or vengeance.

A Shift to the Low Side of Style 2

- You may engage in enabling behavior to make people dependent on you so they will affirm your strength.
- You may manipulate or intimidate others into needing your services in the manner of the Mafia to buttress your own position.
- You use your Godfather or Godmother position for your own aggrandizement vs. for the good of the community.

Style 9
The Peaceful
Person

Positive Descriptors of Your Style

patient
unostentatious
diplomatic
low key
reassuring
modest
objective
unflappable
settled
comfortable

receptive
allowing
permissive
peaceful
in harmony
calm
laissez-faire
easy going
down to earth
few expectations

Negative Descriptors of Your Style

put things off
confluent
indecisive
low energy
distractible
squelch anger
boring
tedious
uncommitted
neglectful

overly adaptable
indolent
passive-aggressive
detached
unresponsive
oblivious
appeasing
unreflective
obstinate
difficulty discriminating

Positive Core Value Tendencies	Distorted Core Characteristics
You value *peace* which is the tranquility of order.	You can overidentify with the *idealized self-image* of being being *settled* and avoid any kind of conflict.
You have an intuitive sense and appreciation for harmony, for when things fit together.	You can overdo agreement. You experience ambivalence about whether to agree or disagree, to conform or not conform.
You possess diplomacy. You are able to reconcile opposing forces and can see both sides of an issue.	You may have difficulty taking a position or choosing sides. You can be indecisive or put off making any decision.
You have an allowing, *laissez-faire* approach to life which encourages people and events to unfold in their own way and at their own pace.	You can assume a passive stance towards life and take the path of least resistance. You can be unassertive and unwilling to intervene on your own behalf. You let things go too long unattended.
You are easygoing and give others freedom and space and let them take the lead.	You can get caught in the dilemma of fearing to express yourself lest you displease others and risk their abandoning you or of feeling resentful because you abandoned yourself and didn't get your needs met.

Positive Core Value Tendencies	Distorted Core Characteristics
You have a calming, reassuring presence.	You may fiddle while Rome burns and refuse to recognize real problems.
You are a non-judgmental, accepting, impartial, and open listener.	You identify so much with others' positions that you may lose touch with or not express your own opinions and preferences.
You can be aware of and attentive to the nuances of each moment.	You have a tendency to generalize, homogenize, and not recognize differences.
You can be in tune with your personal preferences and feelings.	You pay attention to others' feelings but not your own. You can repress and numb out your anger and express it in a passive-aggressive manner.
You have a sense of purpose.	You sometimes believe you don't matter or make a difference.
You are a salt of the earth, down to earth, modest, unassuming person. You are even-tempered and have no need to show off.	You may lack a sense of self-worth and so don't take care of yourself physically, emotionally, socially, intellectually, or spiritually.

Objective Paradigm
Love

Adaptive Cognitive Schema:

You have a sense that you are loved, that you are lovable, and that you are capable of loving.

You are genuinely content with yourself and with reality as it is.

Virtue: *Action*

Adaptive Emotional Schema:

Love wants to pass itself on through action. Gratitude for being loved leads to spontaneous action towards the welfare of the beloved. Action is natural to the real self and works for the development of that self.

When you are in touch with your real self, you know what you need and want and you know what you need to do to get what you want.

The integration of your feelings and thoughts motivate and focus your activity.

Distorting Paradigm
Resignation

Maladaptive Cognitive Schema:

You feel deprived of love and not paid attention to, so you resign yourself, don't let yourself feel or want much, don't let things get to you, and don't make a big deal out of anything.

You can resign yourself to accepting whatever comes your way.

Passion: *Indolence*

Maladaptive Emotional Schema:

Self-doubt and resignation lead to indolence or laziness regarding the growth of oneself and others. Procrastination, indecision, confusion, and inaction arise from the false personality and block action.

When you are inattentive to and neglectful of yourself, you don't know what you need, and so you don't act.

You can distract yourself and diffuse your activity when it comes to doing something really important to you.

Area of Avoidance: *Conflict*

Because you want to be settled, you avoid conflict or anything that would upset you. You pull for agreement and blur differences. You pour oil on troubled waters. You don't hear the squeaks since you want everything to go smoothly.

Defense Mechanism: *Narcoticization*

To avoid conflict you numb your feelings, wants, and preferences. You make everything the same and highlight nothing. You make molehills out of mountains.

How the Distortion of This Style Developed

- You weren't paid attention to enough when you were growing up. You felt neglected and then you neglected yourself.
- Instead of coming to the painful acknowledgement that you weren't loved or cared for or that you apparently didn't matter, you took a less painful stance of resignation by saying, "*It doesn't matter. What's the difference. Why make a big deal out of anything. Life is short.*"
- You turned down your energy, lowered your expectations, and became resigned for the duration.
- You may have grown up in the background, felt overlooked, or overshadowed by your siblings.
- You weren't listened to and so you learned not to listen to yourself. You learned not to pay attention to yourself, your needs, your preferences and wants, your feelings.
- You were caught in the dilemma of confronting others and being abandoned or of conforming to others and being controlled.
- So you took both sides instead of choosing sides. You developed indecision as a conflict-resolution method.
- You experienced a conflict between being good or bad, conformist or non-conformist, agreeing or disagreeing.
- Your solution was not to decide. You learned to postpone, to wait and see, to allow events to take their own course.

- You learned to comfort yourself by setting up a routine and going on automatic pilot.
- Your attempts to express your anger did not meet with success, so you repressed it.

What You Miss as a Result of the Distortion of Your Style

- A sense of accomplishment in getting things done.
- A sense of competency and self efficacy: "*I can do it.*"
- Feeling loved and cared for and in turn being loving and caring.
- A sense of self-worth: "*I really do matter.*"
- A sense of aliveness and vitality.
- The excitement and growth that arise out of conflict.
- A sense of purpose and destiny; you have a place in and a part to play in the unfolding of the universe.

Paradigm Shifts You May Experience
Under Stressful Conditions

A Shift to the Low Side of Your Own Style

- You might say, "*What's the use?*" and become more resigned, more shut down.
- You may avoid confrontation and conflict.
- You may fall asleep, not notice, and not listen instead of dealing with the problem.
- You may become obstinate and unyielding.
- You might avoid even more not taking a position or stating your case.
- Instead of getting organized, you might become more disorganized and therefore unable to act.
- You may procrastinate, put off, and delay more.
- You may become more dependent on others to take care of you.
- You may become overly preoccupied with details and not finish what really needs to get done.

- You might distract yourself by pursuing unimportant, inconsequential matters instead of doing what you need to do.
- You may find yourself sleeping more or daydreaming more.

A Shift to the Low Side of Style 6

- You may become worrisome, fearful, ruminative.
- You may begin to say, "*What if?*" instead of your usual "*So what if?*"
- You may begin making mountains out of molehills.
- You may doubt yourself and your own inner authority and avoid expressing your needs and your position.
- You might begin seeking the approval and affirmation and protection of some outside authority.
- You may become overly responsible and dutiful.
- You could become scrupulous and be overly concerned about keeping the rules and schedule.
- You may stop being relaxed and become rigid and obsessive.

A Shift to the High Side of Style 6

- You can find in yourself the courage to be somebody and take a stand and state your case.
- You can push through your fears of being rejected or ignored, discover what you really want to do and act on those personal desires and preferences.

Paradigm Shifts You May Experience
Under Relaxed Conditions

A Shift to the High Side of Your Own Style

- You can focus and differentiate instead of distracting yourself and becoming confluent.
- You are prompt. You do it now instead of procrastinating.
- You can be assertive. You state your own position, feeling, or preference. You are in touch with your anger and use it to tell you what you want and to enable you to get what you really need.

- You trust your inner authority and resist turning to gurus or other external sources for energy and solutions.
- You are mindful of when you have been loved and touched and cared for. You allow your natural gratitude to lead you to action.
- You are awake to your real self, feelings, and wants. You resist falling asleep and neglecting yourself. You practice mindfulness. You remember yourself vs. being in a trance and forgetting who you are and what you want.
- You take better care of your inner spiritual well-being and your outer physical well-being.
- You don't substitute inconsequentials and nonessentials for what you really need and want.

A Shift to the High Side of Style 3

- You can get focused and goal-oriented. You determine what you want and go get it in a step-by-step manner.
- You become organized and structured from within so you don't have to rely on external pressure to get you moving.
- You aren't just there, you do something. You take action to affect the world. You are in touch with your efficacious self, in touch with the active agent in you instead of being a passive recipient.
- You generate your own energy vs. draining off others' energy.
- You think of yourself as being professional, efficient, and competent.
- You can say to yourself: "*I am successful.*"
- You assume the attitude that you are important, you do matter and make a difference instead of your usual "*It doesn't matter*" or "*I don't matter.*"

A Shift to the Low Side of Style 3

- You may engage in busy work as another way to distract yourself or neglect what you really need to work on.

- You may take on many projects to have something to do instead of intentionally living your own life.
- You may assume a role or some corporate identity and still not know who you are.

Bibliography

BOOKS ABOUT THE ENNEAGRAM

General Introduction

Baron, Renee, and Elizabeth Wagele. *The Enneagram Made Easy.* San Francisco: Harper San Francisco, 1994.

Beesing, Maria, Robert Nogosek, Patrick O'Leary. *The Enneagram: A Journey of Self Discovery.* Denville, NJ: Dimension Books, 1984.

Hurley, Kathleen, and Theodore Dobson. *What's My Type?* San Francisco: HarperCollins, 1991.

_____. *My Best Self: Using the Enneagram to Free the Soul.* San Francisco: HarperSan Francisco, 1993.

Keyes, Margaret. *Emotions and the Enneagram.* Muir Beach, CA: Molysdatur Publ., 1992, Rev. Ed.

Naranjo, Claudio. *Ennea-type Structures.* Nevada City, CA: Gateways/IDHHB,1990.

_____. *Character and Neurosis: An Integrative View.* Nevada City, CA: Gateways, 1994.

Linden, Anné, and Murray Spalding. *The Enneagram and NLP.* Portland, OR: Metamorphous Press, 1994.

Palmer, Helen. *The Enneagram.* San Francisco: Harper and Row, 1988.

_____. *The Enneagram in Love and Work.* New York: HarperCollins, 1995.

Riso, Don Richard. *Personality Types: Using the Enneagram for Self Discovery.* Boston: Houghton Mifflin, 1987.

_____. *Understanding the Enneagram.* Boston: Houghton Mifflin, 1990.

_____. *Discovering Your Personality Type.* Boston: Houghton Mifflin, 1992.

_____. *Enneagram Transformations.* Boston: Houghton Mifflin, 1993.

The Enneagram and Spirituality

Metz, Barbara, and John Burchill. *The Enneagram and Prayer.* Denville, NJ: Dimension Books, 1987.

Nogosek, Robert. *Nine Portraits of Jesus.* Denville, NJ: Dimension Books, 1985.

Rohr, Richard, and Andreas Ebert. *Discovering the Enneagram.* New York: Crossroad, 1990.

_____. *Experiencing the Enneagram.* New York: Crossroad, 1992.

Tickerhoof, Bernard. *Conversion and the Enneagram.* Denville, NJ: Dimension Books, 1991.

Zuercher, Suzanne. *Enneagram Spirituality.* Notre Dame, IN: Ave Maria Press, 1992.

_____. *Enneagram Companions.* Notre Dame, IN: Ave Maria Press, 1993.

Articles and Chapters about the Enneagram

Keen, Sam. "A conversation about ego destruction with Oscar Ichazo." *Psychology Today,* July 1973.

Lilly, John, and Joseph Hart. "The Arica training." *Transpersonal Psychologies.* Ed. Charles Tart. New York: Harper and Row, 1975.

Metzner, Ralph. "The Arica Enneagram of Types." *Know Your Type: Maps of Identity.* New York: Doubleday, 1979.

Wagner, Jerome. "Reliability and validity study of a Sufi personality typology: the Enneagram." *Journal of Clinical Psychology.* 39(5). September 1983.

_____. "The Enneagram and Myers-Briggs: two windows on the self." *New Catholic World.* May/June 1986.

_____. "Comparisons of the Enneagram and Jungian typologies." *Enneagram Educator.* Winter 1990.

_____. "Apologia for the Enneagram and Research." *Enneagram Educator.* Summer, 1994.

Dissertations about the Enneagram

Beauvais, Phyllis. "Claudio Naranjo and SAT: modern manifestation of Sufism." Ph.D., 1973, Hartford Seminary. 35/12-A, p. 8005. GAX 75-13868.

Campbell, Richard. "The relationship of Arica training to self actualization and interpersonal behavior." Ph.D., 1975, United States International University. 36/03-B. GAX 75-20244.

Gamard, William Sumner. "Interrater reliability and validity of judgments of Enneagram personality types." Ph.D., 1986, California Institute of Integral Studies. GAX 86-25584.

Lincoln, Robert. "The relation between depth psychology and protoanalysis." Ph.D., 1983. California Institute of Transpersonal Psychology. Research Abstracts International. LD 00676.

Randall, Stephen. "Development of an inventory to assess Enneagram personality type." Ph.D., 1979. California Institute of Integral Studies. 40/09-B. GAX 80-05160.

Wagner, Jerome. "A descriptive, reliability, and validity study of the Enneagram personality typology." Ph.D., 1981, Loyola University, Chicago. 41/11A. GAX 81-09973.

Wolf, Steven. "Effects of the Arica training on adult development: a longitudinal study." Ph.D., 1985, Saybrook Institute. 46/11B. GAX 85-28854.

Zinkle, Thomas. "A pilot study toward the validation of the Sufi personality typology." Ph.D., 1975, United States International University. 35/05B. GAX 74-24529.

(To order copies, contact *Dissertation Abstracts International,* Dissertion Publishing, University Microfilm International, 300 N. Zeeb Rd., P.O. Box 1764, Ann Arbor, MI 48106; 1-800-521-3042.)

RELATED WORKS

The Arica Tradition

Ichazo, Oscar. *The Human Process for Enlightenment and Freedom.* New York: Arica Institute Press, 1976.

_____. *Between Metaphysics and Protoanalysis*. New York: Arica Institute Press, 1982.

_____. *Interviews with Oscar Ichazo*. New York: Arica Institute Press, 1982.

The Gurdjieff Tradition

Almaas, A.H. *The Elixir of Enlightenment*. York Beach, ME: Samuel Weiser, 1984.

_____. *Essence: the Diamond Approach to Inner Realization*. York Beach, ME: Samuel Weiser, 1986.

_____. *The Void*. Berkeley: Diamond Books, 1986.

_____. *The Pearl Beyond Price*. Berkeley: Diamond Books, 1988.

Bennett, J.G. *Enneagram Studies*. York Beach, ME: Samuel Weiser, 1983.

Campbell, Robert. *Fisherman's Guide*. Boston: Shambhala, 1985.

De Ropp, Robert. *The Master Game*. New York: Dell, 1974.

Ouspensky, P.D. *The Psychology of Man's Possible Evolution*. New York: Vintage, 1974.

Speeth, Kathleen. *The Gurdjieff Work*. Berkeley: And/Or Press, 1976.

Tart, Charles. *Waking Up*. Boston: Shambhala, 1986.

Webb, James. *The Harmonious Circle*. New York: G.P. Putnam's Sons, 1980.

To contact Jerome Wagner for information about
Enneagram workshops and Certification and
Training programs, you can reach him at:

Jerome P. Wagner, Ph.D.
Enneagram Studies and Applications
2603 Broadway
Evanston, IL 60201
(847) 492-1690

About The Author

Dr. Jerome Wagner, Ph.D. is a clinical psychologist and psychotherapist in private practice and at the Counseling Center of Loyola University, Chicago.

One of the original students of the Enneagram in the early 1970s, he has taught graduate courses in the Enneagram for over fifteen years at Loyola's Institute of Pastoral Studies, where he now offers an Enneagram Training and Certification Program.

A witty lecturer and popular speaker, he gives Enneagram workshops in various clinical, academic, business, personal and spiritual growth venues. He has presented the Enneagram at professional conferences of the American Psychological Association and American Counseling Association, and at the First Australian Enneagram Conference in Melbourne. Dr. Wagner was the chairman of the program selection committee and an invited speaker for the First International Enneagram Conference held at Stanford University.

His doctoral dissertation was one of the first to do formal research with the Enneagram and he has been conducting and directing Enneagram research projects ever since.

He is the author of *The Enneagram and the Myers-Briggs: Two Windows on the Self* and *Group Enneagram Styles,* both available on audio cassette.

The exercises in the Introduction are available in a convenient workbook.

If you would like to order a copy, send $2 check or money order and we will send you the workbook postage-paid.

Qty	Title	Price	S/H
_____	**The Enneagram Spectrum of Personality Styles Workbook** Jerome Wagner	$ 2.00	FREE
_____	**Packet of 10 Workbooks**	$15.00	FREE
_____	**The Enneagram Spectrum of Personality Styles** Jerome Wagner	$11.95	4.95*
_____	**The Enneagram Movie & Video Guide** Thomas Condon	$15.95	4.95*
_____	**The Enneagram And NLP** Anné Linden & Murray Spalding	$15.95	5.95#

* Shipping = $4.95 for the first book, $1 for each additional copy
\# Shipping = $5.95 for the first book, $1 for each additional copy

Subtotal for Products		
Subtotal for Shipping		
TOTAL		

If ordering by phone, call toll free
1-800-233-6277

or send check/money order to:
Metamorphous Advanced Product Services (M.A.P.S.)
PO Box 10616
Portland, OR 97210-0616

Metamorphous Press

Metamorphous Press is a publisher of books and other media providing resources for personal growth and positive change. MP publishes leading-edge ideas that help people strengthen their unique talents and discover that we are responsible for our own realities.

Many of our titles center around Neurolinguistic Programming (NLP) and the Enneagram. These are exciting, practical, and powerful models that connect you to observable patterns of behavior and communication and the processes that underlie them.

Metamorphous Press provides selections in many useful subject areas such as communication, health and fitness, education, business and sales, therapy, selections for young persons, and other subjects of general and specific interest. Our products are available in fine bookstores around the world.

Our distributors for North America are:

Bookpeople	Moving Books	the distributors
Ingram	New Leaf	Sage Book Distributors
M.A.P.S.	Pacific Pipeline	

For those of you overseas, we are distributed by:

Airlift (UK, Western Europe)
Specialist Publications (Australia)

New selections are added regularly and availability and prices change, so call for a current catalog or to be put on our mailing list. If you have difficulty finding our products in your favorite bookstore, or if you prefer to order by mail, we will be happy to make our books and other products available to you directly. Please call or write us at:

Metamorphous Press
PO Box 10616 Portland, OR 97210-0616
TEL (503) 228-4972
FAX (503) 223-9117

TOLL FREE ORDERING
1-800-937-7771

METAMORPHOUS
Advanced
Product
Services

METAMORPHOUS ADVANCED PRODUCT SERVICES (M.A.P.S.) is the master distributor for Metamorphous Press and other fine publishers.

M.A.P.S. offers books, cassettes, videos, software, and miscellaneous products in the following subjects: Business/Sales, Children, Education, Enneagram, Health (including Alexander Technique and Rolfing), Hypnosis, Personal Development, Psychology (including Neurolinguistic Programming), and Relationships/Sexuality.

If you cannot find our books at your favorite bookstore, you can order directly from M.A.P.S.

TO ORDER OR REQUEST A FREE CATALOG

MAIL   M.A.P.S.
P.O. Box 10616
Portland, OR 97210-0616

FAX   (503) 223-9117

CALL   Toll free 1-800-233-6277

ALL OTHER BUSINESS

CALL   (503) 228-4972

CPSIA information can be obtained at www.ICGtesting.com
Printed in the USA
BVOW08s2127180516

448552BV00001B/26/P

9 781555 520700